The way my dad left us was what hurt the most . . . It was his third affair (that I know about), and he just left us notes. Mum, my brother and I had been at an archery competition and we came home to three letters and no Dad. I don't think I have ever cried so much. I went to pieces.

Helen Hines worked for seven years at the National Council for One Parent Families, where she produced information for lone parents and jointly managed the Information Team. A published travel writer, she has run several writing workshops, including one for the Federation of Worker Writers, and now has a regular writing group at Walthamstow School for Girls. She loves painting and also works as an illustrator and muralist. In her spare time she helps to run self-development courses.

Family Fallout

Young Women Talk About Family Break-Up

Helen Hines, editor

Livewire

from The Women's Press

First published by Livewire Books, The Women's Press Ltd, 2000
A member of the Namara Group
34 Great Sutton Street, London EC1V 0LQ
www.the-womens-press.com

Collection copyright © Helen Hines 2000

British Library Cataloguing-in-Publication Data
A catalogue record for this book is available from the British Library.

ISBN 0 7043 4956 6

Typeset in 12/14pt Bembo by FiSH Books, London
Printed and bound in Great Britain by Cox &Wyman Ltd,
Reading, Berkshire

For my father, John

Acknowledgements

A big thank you and huge respect to all the writers who bared their souls to talk about their experiences, including those whose pieces are not in this book.

Thank you to all the youth workers and teachers who were enthusiastic about the project and encouraged young people to write, especially to Debbie Upton, Head of English at Walthamstow School for Girls. Thanks to Teresa Garfield who helped out and kept me on track and to the National Council for One Parent Families and Parentline Plus for their help with my search for authors. And finally to Charlotte Cole at The Women's Press who gave me the opportunity to do this book and remained a calm and cheerful steer.

Contents

Introduction

Family break-up is difficult for all involved. It might be the first time we see our parents really upset or angry, and it can be truly disturbing to find that they have their own problems. The fallout affects everyone – especially the children, who usually have no control over the way their life is changing irrevocably.

I was sitting in my office one afternoon at the National Council for One Parent Families when I received a call from The Women's Press saying that they were looking for an editor for a book on family break-up, which would give young women the chance to talk about their experiences. With my background in lone parent publications, I was delighted to be able to say 'yes, I'm the person you're looking for'.

I was also thrilled that at last there would be a resource to help young people cope with family break-up. I hope this book will give the reader a sense that they are not alone and show perhaps that there is a light at the end of the tunnel. Writing for the book has given young women a chance to express themselves and to say what it's really been like – and that includes the good as well as the bad.

At the beginning of the twenty-first century, it is clear that family break-up is more and more common in Britain, with 25 per cent of children now seeing their parents divorce. Surprisingly then, the splitting up of a family is often still seen as out of the ordinary and a sign of failure. Yet families don't stand still. They break up and then get remade in different shapes. Many young people will have lived in a variety of family environments during their childhood and adolescence. Forecasts suggest that the number of stepfamilies will continue to grow. Currently 10 per cent of children live with one natural parent and one step-parent. More and more still will spend some of their life in a one-parent household.

What struck me when reading the pieces was how the contributors' role in the family changed after their parents split up or recoupled. One says she became her parents' personal assistant, another thought she had taken on the role of counsellor, others feel they've had to look after or even rescue their mum or their dad. Many contributors mention that they have become friends with one of their parents. But for some it can always be difficult, especially if the break-up means that they have to go into care.

A child who is left behind will often yearn for the parent who no longer lives at home. This is particularly so when this parent – usually the father – doesn't keep up regular contact. My father died while I was gathering pieces for this book and, even though I'm now in my thirties, my own feeling of loss helped me to realise just how important our parents are. It seems a shame that so many fathers don't realise how much they mean to their children even when they don't live with them any more, especially when these fathers are often feeling left out themselves.

It is clear that children do want their parents to be happy, and do understand that breaking up can be the only way of achieving this. It is inevitably tough for all those involved, but it doesn't have to be as hard as it often is. The contributors have identified things which made it much worse – the shock of only being told at the last minute that their parent was leaving, the tension when they were told, feeling rejected by the parent who left either because of the way they left or because they didn't stay in regular contact, not being able to talk to one or both parents about it afterwards, not being able to express their feelings, having to take matters into their own hands after a period of abusive behaviour.

Getting used to life in a one-parent family or a step-family can be difficult – but it can also be fun. As the contributors in this book show, some feel they have got to know their mum better or developed a closer relationship with other relatives. Others welcome the arrival of stepbrothers and stepsisters – glad that they are no longer the oldest or that they now have a new baby sibling to play with. Some feel they have more quality time with their dad when he isn't living at home. Many have a greater maturity and understanding as a result of the changes. The contributors often have to work at being in a new family set-up – but let's face it, all relationships have to be worked at!

Watching the process that the contributors went through when writing these pieces, it seemed to me that facing the past was always a challenge. Sometimes for the first time, the facts of the break-up fell into place and became clearer, particularly for the young women who had gone through these experiences when very young. It was rewarding for me to give them this space (not just the ones who are included in this book, but all the young women who felt inspired to write on this subject), so that they could somehow explore the fallout – release their pent up feelings and have their point of view heard. One writer said, 'I found writing my feelings down helped me to understand them more and make sense of the confusion that surrounded the situation.' I think this could be a good idea for anyone – just to write it all down and get it out.

Perhaps reading about other people's experiences or even writing down your own could also help you to feel more confident about talking to your parents, siblings, friends (or even a teacher) about what you are going through. When parents are distracted sometimes it's up to us to let someone know what we are feeling. One of the contributors said she wants to send a copy of this book to her father. Even if you just dip into it for an hour, I hope the heartfelt and sometimes humorous stories will help you feel better about your own life and family.

Helen Hines

No Surprises

Bonna Breeze

I'm sitting in the front seat of my mum's car, squashed by my holdall. The boot was rusted and wouldn't open, so I have to have the huge bag by my knees and am beginning to regret having packed quite so much.

I have mixed feelings about going to stay with my dad in Suffolk, as I always do. It's great seeing him, and we always do really fun things, but it seems odd. I never feel like I belong in his flat; I always feel like a short-term guest – which is what I am really, but I don't think it should be like that. I've tried to create my space there, by leaving a dressing gown and soapbag, but it hasn't really worked so far. Also, half the time he treats me as though I'm about 13 rather than 18. If I think about it, it makes sense as he never really saw me growing up. If you added up the amount of time he's spent with me since the divorce, it probably does make me about 13.

I'm not blaming him for not being there, you understand, but it's different for us. A lot of my friend's parents who've split up still live close by, so they see them all the time. Our dad lives at the other end of the country, and we have to make detailed arrangements to see him. This usually means phone calls with me relaying messages back and forth:

'So how about on Saturday?'

'Dad says how about Saturday? Hang on, no, I've got my Saturday job. Sunday?'

'Fine.'

'Dad says Sunday's fine.'

'That's fine by me, too. Shall we meet at 12?'

'Mum says meet at 12.'

'I can't make it till one.'

'Dad can't make it till one.'

'Tell him one's fine.'

'One's fine.'

And so on.

But mainly it's worth it; and I do like spending time with him. His place has a very different atmosphere to the one back home in Yorkshire, which is an all-girl household. That's a lot of fun – we've got a poster of Brad Pitt on the bathroom door, and Ewan McGregor on the inside of the cereal cupboard. Then, of course, there's the standard war cry round the dinner table of 'Boys? Urgh, yuck!' when someone mentions the dreaded males. When I think of the way we live, I tend to think of a lot of laughter – well, giggles, more to the point. My mum can appreciate my dirty jokes! But she's always good for advice, too. I think I'm closer to her because of the divorce than I would otherwise have been – I can tell her pretty well anything and she won't freak. As I get older, I'm starting to feel a lot more on a level with her; almost like an equal partner sometimes. Of course, other times she makes it very clear that I'm not. That makes it a bit hard to tell where I stand.

It's similar with my dad, actually. When he's not treating me like a thirteen-year-old, he treats me as a grown-up – which is good. The trouble is he confides in me – about his money problems, work problems, life problems and so on, and they then feel like my responsibility. I can't really tell my mum about them because she's not interested; I can't tell my sister because she's too young to understand; and it's completely irrelevant to anyone outside the family.

'We're he-re!' yells my sister from the back seat.

'Here' is a service station on the A1, where we meet up, about halfway between the two houses. As we pull into the car park, I can see his car is already here, parked in the usual spot. My sister tumbles first out of the car and runs across the car park. 'Daddeee!' she squeals, flinging herself at him. I follow soon after, grinning as he grabs us both in a huge bear hug.

After we've got over the meeting and greeting ceremony, it's time to decide whether we're staying for a cup of tea or not. Apparently, today we are. As we troop in the café, my sister is hanging from my dad's arm and I'm walking with my mum. In these situations I'm always very conscious of my mum, even though she always stays very quiet. I feel like I need to look after her and not desert her – I'll have plenty of time with my dad at his flat. My sister never seems to pick up on things like this, which is hardly surprising because she's only 12.

Once we're inside, I have to think about seating arrangements on a table for four. My parents can't sit on the same side of the table. Not that they'd argue or make a scene – far from it. The atmosphere would just be very cold and uninterested, and pretty uncomfortable for all of us.

They tend not to have much to do with each other, even in situations like this, which means it doesn't feel like we're all in the same group. Rather, there are two groups – me, my sister and my mum, or me, my sister and my dad – that don't mix with each other. Both parents tend to bring up 'in-jokes' that they have with me and my sister, as though to shut out the other or show how much better they get on with us. We're stuck in the middle, being careful never ever to look like we're taking sides. There's so much for us to consider!

So here we are, sitting around a table, all being incredibly polite to one another and drinking tea. We're obviously staying a little longer than usual today, as we've ordered toasted teacakes. My dad tries to start a conversation.

'So, girls, what have you been doing with yourselves?'

'Not much. Working.'

'I tidied my room.'

We'd like to talk – a conversation would be far better than polite silence – it's just that the words suddenly aren't there. Now it's my mum's turn.

'You'll be good for your dad, won't you, girls?'

'Yep.'

'Yep.'

We all stir our tea intently.

The four teaspoons clink loudly.

Outside it starts to rain.

'You'll be all right driving the girls in this, won't you?' This was from my mum.

'Of course, we'll be fine, won't we? And you?'

'Yes, fine.'

We go back to tea stirring. Neither of my parents seem to trust the other's driving skills much, and asking about driving conditions always seems to take up a good deal of conversation.

The toasted teacakes arrive, slightly burnt, and we can all occupy ourselves with buttering them. I decide to have a go with speech.

'Even I don't burn these!'

This attempt at light-heartedness sounded far wittier in my head, and barely raises a smile from anyone.

Silence can make people say the stupidest things. I once read about a survey someone did to see how long people will put up with an uncomfortable silence before coming out with something pointless. I think the average was about seven seconds. Obviously the participants weren't provided with tea to stir at the same time.

We finish our teacakes and stand up to leave. Back outside, we run back and forth between the two cars, transferring luggage and getting wet. Once we've finished, my sister settles herself fast in the back of my dad's car, arranging her books and toys around her. Her goodbye is conducted through the open window, to prevent anything falling out. I give my mum a huge hug and tell her to be good before she gets a chance to tell me the same! I realise I'm getting drenched, and hurry into my dad's car. My sister, desperate for the last word, reaches out for another hug through the window, then Dad starts the car and we're off. We keep waving to Mum all the way out of the car park and around the roundabout until she reaches her turning, and only then do we feel we're on the way again.

This is so much more relaxed than in the café. Now we can have the in-jokes and they don't feel exclusive any more; I don't feel guilty. It's always the same; relaxed when we're with one parent but tense when we're with both. And, of course, when they're tense, we're tense.

But it's okay now. We're going to my dad's and that's always fun. I shove my Radiohead tape in the car stereo (Mum says they sound suicidal, but Dad never criticises my choice in music), and my favourite track 'No Surprises' fills the car. We drive off into the rain. Looks like it might clear up later.

Visiting Times

Monique Ferguson

As I lie on my hospital bed, I hear the buzzer go. This means visitors, which, believe me, is about the most exciting thing that happens when you're in a place like this. My heart quickens, first with anticipation, but then with dread. What if it's my mum? My dad is due soon and if they both come together it will be a complete nightmare. Don't get me wrong, I love both my parents to bits and I wouldn't change them for the world, but it's one of the most awkward positions I have ever been in and it is repeated over and over again. They arrive and they make excuses to be somewhere else and leave me alone again. Or I become a personal assistant, organising both of them.

'Right, Dad. Mum and David (that's my stepdad) are coming in to see me at about eight o'clock.'

'Okay,' he says, 'I'll pop in after work, about four.'

'Right,' I say, feeling more and more like a PA.

I go into hospital quite a lot and it's nice to have visitors, it's a time of normality for me – in hospital I feel like I'm shut away from the rest of the world. I just wish that they could have some sort of spontaneity when they visit, like my boyfriend or friends who pop in when they feel like it. I know that both my parents have plenty of other responsibilities besides me, but it would be nice if they could just put aside their differences and be with me. I am not naïve enough to believe that this could happen but it's nice to let the imagination out for a run now and again.

The reason that I am in hospital may not sound much but it's something that totally rules my life and it's getting worse. Asthma – I hate that word, rather like the way I used to hate the word Divorce and all that it brought. I come into hospital every couple of months for a week or two because I have very bad attacks and I end up attached to drips, monitors and God knows what else. The sense that everything is caving in and the frustration and the mixed emotions that an attack bring are like the feelings I had when my dad first left. I couldn't control what was happening and I was scared because I couldn't really influence the outcome.

Plenty of my friends have parents who are divorced and know exactly what I am going through. It's like living two different lives, one with Mum and one with Dad. I have to watch what I say and it's very difficult to adjust. I used to get moody when I came back from my dad's house, but I feel that I have matured since then.

Dad had threatened to leave before but I begged him to stay, so he did. This was one of the worst mistakes I have ever made. When I see how happy my parents are now – with their new partners – I realise that this is the best situation for everyone.

In a way, I am lucky. I have two families and two houses. I am welcome at both and I have plenty of people to turn to for comfort and advice. Christmas and birthdays are also good; two lots of presents, food and fun. The split has made me stronger in one way, but very vulnerable in many others. I find it difficult to trust people and to let them get close to me because I am scared of being hurt again. But I think it's been the type of hurt that (thankfully) you can only experience once in your life.

I don't think that she means to, but my mum sometimes makes me feel guilty for going to see my dad. So I sometimes lie about where I have been because I think the truth hurts her more. I can understand the reasons why, but her behaviour still makes me very wary.

Another problem I have is my part-time job. It's in a major superstore, which is local to both my families, and I have often had to usher my dad out when my mum is there too. I do sometimes feel that I'm in the middle and this is definitely not a nice feeling to have. I am often jealous of my friends whose parents are still together, especially if they do not appreciate what they have.

Since the marriage break-up, I have met some people who have influenced my life greatly. The major one is Wesley Price, my counsellor, who has made me see that it's not the end of the world and that, just because my parents' relationship has broken down, it doesn't mean that mine with either of them has to. Other people are the friends I have made at sixth-form college, especially Katie, Liz and Scott, without whom I don't think I would be the person I am today. I have come to realise that friends are equally as important as family, just for different reasons. Friends will be there for you when your family can't, and they don't take sides. They are there for me and I hope I am there for them too.

The way my dad left was what hurt the most, that and the betrayal. It was his third affair (that I know about), and he just left us notes. Mum, my brother and I had been at an archery competition and we came home to three letters and no Dad. I don't think that I have ever cried so much. I went to pieces. A couple of months later I was contemplating what life would be like for everyone else if I wasn't here any more. A large bottle of pills in my hand, already half empty. That was my cry for help, that was when I met Wesley. He was my saviour and I learnt a lot about myself during the time I spent with him. He made me realise that I was important and should start considering myself for a change. I now enjoy being me; I actually like myself and I have started having fun. I know now that I can count on my friends, and that one of my mistakes before was not talking, I bottled everything up. Now, if I can't talk, I'll write my feelings down and show my friends. They can help me then and their support and kindness has been invaluable. I can be me and that's what they like me for.

Being in hospital has made me realise that there are plenty of other people who have far more problems than I can ever know, and that they also make the best of whatever life they may have. I have always been determined that I won't live in the past and that I will always look to the future for guidance.

A nurse has just walked past my room (lucky me, they've given me my own one this time instead of a bed on the main ward). I was hoping to go home tomorrow but it's not going to happen because I had a bad turn last night. I realise the pressure that me being in hospital puts on my mum and dad and the rest of both of my families, and if I could change the circumstances I would. But it seems that fate has dealt most of the dud cards to me and my family. I also seem to have a problem standing up without falling over and breaking my wrist, which I've just done again for about the fifth time in two years (I hadn't touched a drop – the normal reason for my loss of balance).

After my visitor, it'll be almost time for dinner and I wonder what delights they have in store for us tonight. I usually beg Dad to bring me in something edible (although he seems to think fast food is anything but, I can't imagine why). I suppose the visits and the food are another way for me to keep in touch with what's going on outside – it's important for me to know what's going on, I'm afraid of being left behind. That was another thing I didn't like about the split: the not knowing what was going on and the uncertainty about what would happen to my family. How would we manage and what we would do if we couldn't? I wasn't worried just for me but also for my brother and for my mum, both of whom were vulnerable at the time. I thought I hated my dad, but I don't believe anyone is really capable of that emotion and I regard it as a very ugly word. It's taken time to forgive him, and although I don't think that our relationship is the same as it was, I really enjoy the time that I get to spend with him and I know that I love him.

The person who was responsible for the buzzer and my raised pulse has just walked past the window and my heart takes a leap. It's my boyfriend and his visits fill me with joy. I love spending time with him and he's very patient and understanding towards me. He is everything I was looking for. In fact, everyone in my life is all that I am looking for. I am a very lucky eighteen-year-old to have had the rich experiences which have filled my life up till now. Long may they last.

Homesick

Sara Jenkins

When my parents told me and my older brother that they were separating, it instantly made me feel sick. That feeling stayed with me for months afterwards – even now it comes back, triggered by different things.

That day I knew something strange was going on because my older brother had come back home from London for the day and my dad was back for the weekend. Both Mum and Dad looked kind of tense and Mum was crying a little and Dad hugged her.

I said to Mum, 'If you're about to tell me something bad, don't, because you'll spoil my trip.' (I was going on a football tour to the Isle of Man with the university football team.)

Mum just said, 'Oh, Sara,' and looked at me with tears in her eyes.

I was sitting in the living room facing them both, the

tears were welling up inside me and a sick 'butterflies' feeling crept in. I don't remember which one said it but I heard, 'We are going to separate.'

I never ever thought I'd hear those words from my parents. At first I didn't believe it, but the tears started to stream down my face and I felt a huge hole plunge into my stomach. Part of this was from seeing a single tear roll down my dad's cheek and the expression of pain on his face. My mum was upset as well and I now realise that it was probably one of the hardest things they had ever done.

My brother reacted coldly. I guess this was his way of dealing with it. I don't remember much about the rest of the day, except that my brother drove me into the next valley and we walked up it and sat down. He put his arm around me and told me everything would be okay and that we had to just accept it because it was what they wanted.

I was in a state of panic; I didn't understand. Throughout my whole life my parents had been together, they'd hardly ever argued. I thought they were the perfect couple, that they would always be together. It was something I had taken for granted, which made it worse. Nothing could have prepared me for the impact of it.

My dad had been a mature student at Manchester University for three years, and part of that time was spent abroad in Egypt and Spain. When he was in Manchester he would come home on weekends. I had just gone to university myself and so hadn't noticed that Dad had stopped coming back home. I guess I was too wrapped up in my new life to see what was happening.

The worst thing was that I had had this sick feeling

before, when I got homesick as a child, and the only way that I could feel better was by being with my parents. They made me feel safe, like nothing could hurt me and that they would always be there for me. Now I felt that sickness again and they couldn't make it better because they were the ones who had caused it.

It took a long time to get rid of the emptiness that filled me that day, and I still sometimes feel it. I've tried to fill it with all sorts of things – boyfriends, drugs, friends – but the only thing that helped was time and knowing my parents were still there for me, just separately. But even thinking about the pain brings back a small feeling of emptiness and tears.

At first, I was angry with both of them for just giving up on 27 years of marriage. Marriage doesn't seem an adequate word for 27 years of life together, all those experiences and emotions, all the problems they overcame, two children, the death of their own parents. I can't describe adequately what they must have been through together; their whole adult lives spent with each other – and they just gave up – well, that's how I saw it. Instead of being the bright, happy, energetic eighteen-year-old I had been, I felt like I had the weight of the world on my shoulders. My veil of illusion had been pierced and I began to resent everyone. I even resented myself for being so naïve. My cynicism appeared without me realising; I was out with three of my friends, we had just seen *Romeo and Juliet*, one of the greatest love stories of all time, and as I walked out of the cinema I said as loudly as I could, 'If they had lived they would have got divorced anyway.' And that's how I felt, because the two people I thought were the most in love, and who would never split up, had let me down and I just couldn't understand. If they couldn't make it through no one could.

I took on the role of counsellor. No one had really explained why my parents had separated. Mum just said she couldn't cope with the depressive, tired side of Dad that had taken over. She said, 'He was always different with you, he always made sure you didn't see him when he was tired and depressed.' I didn't think they had discussed it properly or they would have got back together.

When I asked my dad he didn't seem to know why they'd split up or didn't want to discuss it – he found it hard to accept that he was as much to blame as Mum. So I took it upon myself to try and sort it out. I couldn't stand by and let them throw it all away, but I think I just made matters worse.

I began to ask Mum something, and pick up on certain stuff, and then would talk to Dad and repeat what Mum had said. Dad would then answer – and I'd go back to Mum – and so it went on until they started to get defensive and it was horrible.

One particular time Mum had said, 'Henry didn't even want to go to marriage guidance counselling.' This really angered me because I thought he had wanted to save the marriage. Dad had moved to Spain, so I carried this with me until I went to visit him some months later, and then one night I said, 'Why didn't you want to go to counselling?'

He got angry with Mum. 'She had no right to say that. I went along to a session and the counsellor just took Mum's side immediately.'

I just didn't know who to believe or what to believe. I felt like I couldn't trust them and started to feel like I was the adult and alone in all of it – the two people who I loved and respected the most were lying to me and arguing through me. I'd made the mistake of putting my parents on a pedestal – of thinking they were super-human and not realising they were just human like the rest of us.

After this, my anger and confusion began. I needed someone to blame and my mum got it full blast. She was the one who had instigated the divorce, and according to Dad it was as much a shock to him as it was to me. I felt very resentful that she had given up on Dad, and had taken the easy way out. Every time I saw my dad I felt his pain. I'd never seen him like that before, he used to be an energetic, joker Dad who laughed a lot. And now I saw a tired, unhappy person who just looked so drained. One time he came to pick me up from the airport after I'd been to Australia to stay with a friend and I was on top of the world. When I saw Dad he looked so empty – I started to feel sick again – and I blamed Mum.

I rang her almost straight away and shouted, 'I'm really angry with you for what you've done to Dad.'

I really felt hate for what she had caused, but I was just using her as someone to blame. It was really hard to see my dad like this; what I didn't realise was this is how Mum had seen him for years before they separated and she thought the split would be best in the long run for both of them – including Dad. She kept saying, 'I'm giving Dad wings.'

It was about two years after they split up that I found out my dad had a new partner. I didn't find out from my dad, it was my brother's girlfriend who accidentally said something. I immediately said, 'Oh not Dad, Dad doesn't have a girlfriend.' She then realised I hadn't been told and quickly covered up her blunder, but I knew something was up and when I spoke to Dad, he told me. I was happy for him, and also glad that he lived in another country so I didn't have to have it shoved in my face. I was happy he found someone he could be with, but I wasn't ready to see them together. I wondered how Mum would feel when she found out. I guess I was still hoping they would get back together.

I can admire Mum now for being so courageous; it must have been the hardest thing she has ever done in her life. I know a lot of my friends' parents who argue and want to split up, but they don't because they are frightened of what might happen. My mum is now doing what she has always wanted to do – practising nutrition and she is living in a beautiful cottage in the countryside. And my dad is living in a beautiful *chosa* on the southernmost tip of Spain, doing what he has always wanted; being creative, writing, drawing and soaking up the sun.

A book I read during the time of the divorce (*Living in the Light* by Shakti Gawain) helped me understand what I was going through. My whole outlook on life changed because of the divorce. For a while I was very depressed and cynical, but then I realised if I want to live then I have to get up and do things instead of feeling sorry for myself. I saw that if I want to be happy and achieve what I want to in this life there is no time to be depressed and cynical. Life throws things at you and you can either sit down and take it or you can stand up and grab it with both hands.

My relationship with my brother changed as a result of the divorce as well. He doesn't talk about it much but it meant that we had something to deal with together, and that has brought us a lot closer. It's also made me understand that I will be okay no matter what happens, and that my parents will be there for me always wherever they are or whoever they are with.

Daddy's Girl?

Rebecca Woollard

The way my parents broke the news of their divorce to me and my brother set the tone for the chaotic nature of the early days of their separation. They chose not to tell us until ten o'clock on the night before my dad was set to move out, midway through an episode of *A Bit of a Do*. My mum told me to turn the TV off, which I did, presuming she didn't want us to watch it because it was too rude. Even after she'd said the ominous, 'We've got something to tell you,' I still didn't understand the awesome nature of what was to come. I remember running out of the room in tears and my dad coming into my room to recite the usual clichés: 'This doesn't mean I love you any less' and 'We'll still see lots of each other.' But I don't remember a lot considering it was such an important and formative moment in my life.

What we weren't told was that my dad was moving in

with the woman he'd been having an affair with (now his wife). Or that, despite his promises, we would only see him once a week for a few painful hours, when he would come to our house and sit on the sofa lecturing us about the history of World War Two and his job rather than talk about anything personal. He was so extreme in this way that he didn't manage to tell us he had remarried until a year after the event, claiming that he had forgotten to mention it. Unfortunately, this seems to be a character trait I've inherited from him, although to a lesser extent.

In the end, it was my mum who felt obliged to tell us about Dad's girlfriend, because we wanted to call Dad and she didn't want us to have to deal with the shock of a woman answering. She has never been a big part of our lives. When we did eventually meet, we got on all right. I've never really had a chance to get to know her properly but the fact that she never wants to have children has made me dislike her a little. She hasn't tried to play the role of stepmother – which I appreciate – and has always been friendly. But I have always felt that she didn't consider us part of the package when she married my dad, which we should be. I think the problem is that she was very cautious when she met me, and to some extent still is, because she expected me to dislike her. After all, I am close to my mother and very similar to her. My loyalty to my mum does put a strain on our relationship. My grandma, on my mum's side, has also made the relationship between myself and my dad and his wife difficult. She dislikes them both (for obvious reasons) and makes her opinion known. Luckily, the divorce hasn't affected my relationship between my dad's family and my mum or us. We visited my grandad several times before he died. We also still see some other members of his family.

However, the knock-on effects of my parents' divorce are immense. It has changed my relationship with my dad completely. I feel real anger towards Dad because of his affair, the way things were withheld and the way in which I felt abandoned by him, particularly when he moved to New Zealand. As a child I was a real 'daddy's girl', we were very close, but now on occasions I feel I mean little to him. Despite my fairly bitter tone, it has actually been ten years since my parents divorced. My dad emigrated to New Zealand four years ago. I visit occasionally (six weeks in four years), but it is difficult, at least for me, although my dad doesn't seem aware of any problems.

What saddens me the most is that he won't recognise there is a problem with our relationship. After I found out that he had remarried and not told us, I didn't speak to him for several months, yet he never made an effort to contact me so that we could talk about it. Eventually the strain of having to leave the house every week when he was coming round grew too much and things returned to normal without us once discussing the issue. I think it is probably the lack of communication I have with my father, not the quantity but the quality, which makes my parents' divorce so painful for me, even after so many years.

I am also angry that he seems to have had none of the problems, hurt or anger that I have felt and that he does not recognise that he has caused me any pain. I know deep down that he must be aware that ours is not a normal father-daughter relationship and that he is missing out as much as I am, but he just never mentions it. I doubt he ever will. I find it very hard to hear him when he's on the phone, talking about my brother and speaking as though he knows him as well or better than I do. I also think an acknowledgement that something was wrong would mean he cared about the state of our relationship.

Although I have discussed all this many times with my mum, who is very supportive and non-judgemental, the person I need to talk it through with really is, literally and metaphorically, thousands of miles away. I have written so many imaginary letters to him and had hundreds of conversations with him in my head but to speak the words seems impossible. I think what I need to tell him most is that I feel he has abandoned me, as if the fact that I live in the UK is not enough to keep him here. Even 10 years on I'm really angry that I haven't been able to shout at him.

In comparison to some fathers it may seem that he's done nothing so very awful, but he has hurt me and changed the way I see things and deal with people. He has made me cynical about relationships. I have to fight hard not to become clingy and needy, constantly thinking that I'm going to be left. I also have a tendency to expect the worst from people, especially boyfriends. If my boyfriend has to cancel an evening we had planned to spend together, I often assume it is because he is seeing someone else or that I am somehow at fault or have done something wrong, which is not the case. I think I am always going to be a little untrusting and possessive of the people I love because of my dad leaving.

I have thought about cutting him out of my life

altogether by not visiting or speaking to him, but the prospect of losing him permanently seems worse and I'm not even sure it would help. I look at friends whose fathers are no longer alive and feel incredibly selfish and guilty. I feel as though I should make the most of having a dad, even if we don't get on that well. Obviously our relationship is too complex for me to simply hate him. I see a lot of myself in him and am constantly made aware, when I speak to him, of the link between us, which I wouldn't want to lose.

Maybe I can send him this book.

My World, My Playground

Zaynah Farsian

As I sit watching children tease and play with each other on this warm summer afternoon I feel a sense of envy steal over me; they display a happiness I yearned for as a child, but never had.

My father came here from India in 1979. My mother was born in Mauritius – but her parents came from India – and she had been living in Britain since the age of five. As was common in those days, marriages between families were based on trust, a trust my grandparents honestly believed in. In our case, with my mother's grandmother and my father's father being first cousins, how could things possibly go wrong?

Although my father's immediate family was in India, he had a number of close relatives in England.

One of these was my father's uncle. He was a self-proclaimed priest of the local mosque. I say 'self-proclaimed' because the mosque, to my knowledge, never gave him any training, nor did they acknowledge him as a priest. He was a man who could do no wrong, but was always the first to criticise others.

We were sent to his house for our Islamic teachings every weekday, and it was here that I overheard his family say what they really thought of my mother. In their opinion, my mother didn't know how to look after her husband, her children and her house and they said she needed to be browbeaten into submission. We had a number of gatherings when my father's mother came to visit us from India. On one occasion, I overheard her tell her sister that my mother was lazy and a bad cook. According to them she lacked what they thought were all the essential qualities of a wife. I told my mother everything I had heard them all saying behind her back.

My father must have told his uncle what I'd said. When I next went to have my lessons I was summoned to see him immediately. It was the most humiliating day of my life. There were approximately thirty students in the room. I was scared, and being a quiet, obedient child I felt extremely nervous standing in front of everyone. He called me closer. I gazed at him unaware of what was to happen next, when suddenly I felt his huge hand collide aggressively with my face. He yelled and told me that I was not supposed to report back any of his family's discussions to my mother or her family.

Over the years, my father and his uncle became what I called the Hitler's army. The uncle was a reincarnation of Hitler, my father – Hitler's general. Everything my father did, from getting a job to moving house, had to be done with his uncle's approval, but he never consulted my mother or us children. We survived on the bare minimum, while his mother laid marble in her house in India.

I gradually realised that my father's and my uncle's teachings were not truly in keeping with the Qur'an. They twisted everything to their favour, to back up all their efforts to manipulate and control us.

They refused to allow us the freedom to develop as children. They gave themselves the right to beat their wives into submission. As children, we were tormented to see the mother we adored so weakened by fear, afraid of doing something wrong that would provoke my father's anger. Looking back, I cannot remember him ever being content with anything my mother did – except giving birth to a son.

Being the oldest of four, I can clearly remember the day my brother was born. My father came home ecstatic. I had never seen him like this before. His long-awaited son had arrived – the heir that would carry his name. My sister was born two years previously and I can remember his lack of enthusiasm because she was just another girl. It is common among the Asian community for girls, when they marry, to go to live with their new family. My brother would stay on with my father and later inherit everything he owned.

My father never spent much money on any of us, and we wore clothes donated by friends and my mother's family, but my brother had it much easier. Father would be more inclined to buy gifts for him than for us girls. But it was in India, in the village surrounded by my father's family, that I noticed how lucky my brother was to be a boy. He was given hundreds of rupees to spend in a single day and would be offered rides in my uncles' cars, while us girls had to stay at home. The only place where we felt equal was with my mother's family, who also lived in the village. They were extremely loving and caring to each of us. They showed me how people from the same village can be very different – that surroundings do affect people, but it's upbringing that separates individuals. My father's behaviour did not reflect the village and its people as I had previously thought; but, perhaps, it did reflect a twisted childhood. I would watch my mother's cousin come home and play, talk and joke with his family, and would compare him to us – living in fear as six o'clock approached, the time when my father would walk through the door, and life ruled by dictatorship would begin again.

My parents were married for 13 years, and from this time I can recall several painful events. One occasion that stands out as if it was yesterday was when the fun fair came to town. We managed to build up the courage to ask my father to take us, and were astonished when he agreed. We were so happy that we threw caution to the wind and forgot that my father never did anything without an ulterior motive. During the drive to the fair, my sisters and I carefully planned which rides we would go on.

Arriving at the fair, we ran for the bumper cars first. We were laughing – just like other children – but surprisingly for us because it was not like us to be so free in our father's presence. I turned and ran up to him and said, 'Thank you, Daddy, for bringing us. The bumper car costs forty pence. Can we go on it, please?'

Only to have him reply, 'I didn't bring you all here to waste my money.'

We spent the next 40 minutes wandering around the fun fair watching others enjoy themselves. We didn't go on any rides. It was all to show us that my father was the man of the house and that what he said goes. I can't think of words that express the hollow feeling I experienced as I watched everyone else having fun.

Over the next few years, things deteriorated rapidly, and the only stability we had was from my grandfather – my mother's father. In the fifties, when his father's cloth business collapsed, my grandfather came to England. We learnt a lot from him. As an honest, loving and truly religious man, he showed us a different path to life. He was continually battling with my father and disagreed with his ideas. All he wanted was for his daughter and grandchildren to be happy and content. My father hated him for showing us an alternative way of life that involved not only religion but the world as well. After his death my father's attitude changed for the worse as there was no longer another man to confront him.

My father came to my mother a few months after my grandfather's death, and asked if she would agree to him marrying a second time. For once, my mother replied with a sudden burst of confidence, 'Divorce me first.' She sounded almost smug.

My mother and my father fought many battles over the next two years. He was adamant that *he* would not waste his money on a divorce, so went on a mission to persuade my mother to divorce him. He taunted her, saying that she would be the one to die before him. He made numerous attempts to kill her; one evening he plunged her head in water and held her there – when he released her it was only to carry on his shouting.

My father's physical and mental abuse was targeted specifically at my mother, but at times he'd argue with anyone. We gradually learnt how to read the warning signs, and when and how to avoid a confrontation. Out of all of us it is probably me and my sister who remember what actually happened, the other two were too young. However, in general, I feel it has made me stronger and more independent. If we had been weaker or if my mother's family had been less supportive, maybe we wouldn't have all come out of it unscathed.

Fate intervened in January 1994 when my father decided that it was about time my mother was taught a new lesson, and that the only way to do this was with his fists. We were downstairs preparing for prayers when he came in and ordered my mother upstairs. All we could hear were cries from the bedroom, and all I could think of was if he had plunged her head under water before, what would he do to her now – kill her? He'd no doubt remarry again, but what would we do without our beloved mother? Unable to stand the cries for help any longer I took matters into my own hands and phoned the police. I was thirteen years old. It was the scariest move I had ever made. It took immense courage. I was going against my father and his laws, one of which was never to betray him.

For months up until the court case, I lived in fear that my father would return to get me. My mother did not ask for a divorce, but he was now facing charges for actual bodily harm. My father was found guilty, and hot on the heels of the court case were the divorce papers that he had applied for...freeing us all.

Now, as an adult, I try rationalising the behaviour of a grown man, a husband and a father. I try to find answers that will justify how a man could be so cruel. I'm sure it has something to do with his family and his upbringing. He was an attention seeker, in need of grandeur, and gained this superior feeling by controlling our lives. I pity him – it has lost him his family.

Six years on, we have learnt so much as a family. My grandmother (my mother's mum) has taught us unity, love, respect and confidence in ourselves. My mother especially has gained so much confidence since my father left, doing things she never had the courage to do before. She is loving and caring and so full of life. She can be quiet when need be and voice her opinions when the occasion arises. Both my mother and my grandmother constantly stress the importance of balancing worldly needs and religion. We have been encouraged to do so many things – to have friends, to go out, to understand why we need an education – but most of all we've been taught to use this painful experience to learn and to make us better people and, hopefully, decent parents one day. We have been taught the beauty of Islam; we have been encouraged not to recite Arabic scriptures but to understand the meaning of life, and how families are really meant to be full of love and harmony. My father's teachings are now something of the past, as he is. We have no contact with him. We live with our mother and her family, who take a genuine interest in our lives.

We are all free. Now I no longer watch the children play in envy, as I can now be a child in this world's playground.

Little Miss Invincible

Isaaka Wesley

On 5 September 1995 I, Isaaka Wesley, aged 11, was moved into a children's home in north London. Why? I finally stood up to my physically and sexually abusive father and reported him to the NSPCC. After I gave information about myself over the phone they were soon able to track me down, and Social Services came to remove me from the house. I remember that day well. I was in floods of tears as the social workers escorted me out of the house along with three black bags filled with but a fraction of my belongings. My stepmother later told me that the rest of my belongings had been burnt. She was really angry with me for informing the NSPCC and said I should have told her and she would have found another solution. She'd appeared on the scene with her son when I was seven. She was one of Dad's many girlfriends, but the only one he married. She was the brainiest one – she helped me with my schoolwork and I'd always thought she was a strong, intelligent woman.

At the home, I always seemed to stand out. At the beginning I was the only black kid there. Then, as more black kids moved in, I was the oversensitive black kid. Then I was too posh. I was ridiculed and humiliated for being smart. So I bunked school a few times and I began to swear, bully and criticise just to fit in. It became clear to people that I was a disturbed child. I suffered the most bewildering mood swings. I used to do crazy things for attention, like fainting or pretending to be sick, crying on purpose or running away for the thrill of knowing that someone, somewhere would be worrying about me. I was eleven years old and I felt like I had no one.

During the six months that I was in the home, contact with my stepmother was rare. There were no calls, no letters, no birthday or Christmas cards. During one visit from her, shortly after my twelfth birthday, I did receive the most awful pair of vivid green and yellow inline skates. I only kept them the short while that I did for sentimental reasons. My stepmother approved of the home. I think 'cosy' was the word that she used to describe it. But I didn't care whether or not she approved – I didn't care what she thought about anything. She'd failed me as a mother, abandoned me. She'd broken the strong bond that I thought we shared. She wasn't even my real mother, why should I expect her to be loyal?

My real mother has no idea what's happened to me. I was brought over from Jamaica by my father when I was nine months old. My mother was supposed to follow us but, the story goes, when she found out my father had slept with her best friend she decided not to come. She has remained in Jamaica ever since and, my father being the man he is, I don't blame her.

Playing Little Miss Invincible was cracking me up. I'd finally realised that I was only human, and a twelve-year-old can't carry the whole world on her shoulders. I attempted to commit suicide on several occasions. I tried to strangle myself with ties, sashes and even bras. All these items were removed and the night staff were instructed to sit outside my bedroom with the door open. I couldn't seem to handle not having any family around me any more. Then I made another suicide attempt. This time it was an overdose. I was rushed to hospital immediately and forced to drink a bottle of charcoal. On my first night in hospital I gave my stepmother a call in the hope that she'd come and visit. I could hear the clamour of one of my father's parties in the background. I tried to sound desperately lonely and afraid but I think I just came across as pathetic. I explained to her what I'd done. She said she would phone me, but she didn't sound bothered. Although I gave her the name and address of the hospital she never did call or visit.

I was then given a counsellor – Jonathan. He was young, funny and easy to talk to. It always seemed like he understood, and maybe that was because he did. I soon started to pick myself up and clear my head. I set new goals and began to think for myself. I was on my own but doing fine.

A year later I was living with foster parents and things were going really well. Then my stepmother came back on the scene. She'd had enough of my father now and wanted me back. I didn't want to leave my foster home but felt I couldn't say no to her. This messed me up big time. It seemed that the more involved she became in my life the more I rebelled. I'd turned out bright, ambitious and independent, but it was everyone else who'd been left to bring me up. Why should I become her model daughter now?

Well, I wasn't having any of it. A group of older, white teenagers I'd been hanging around with became a vital part of my life. They were into drugs, alcohol and sex. I joined in but only with the drink. We used to have a lot of fun roaming the streets completely slashed out of our brains – singing, play fighting and intimidating other passers-by. Sometimes I'd sit and watch them inhaling aerosols – they would get all hyper and giggly. I never saw them take any hard drugs although they often told me what it was like to be on a trip. It wouldn't have taken much to persuade me to start taking drugs, but one of the boys wouldn't even let me try smoking. I appreciated him for protecting me. I ran away with these friends twice but then my stepmother laid down the law again.

Within a year I was in south London living with her and a tight curfew. I fitted into my new school very smoothly and my grades were cool – As, Bs and the occasional C. I still felt a lot of anger and bitterness towards my stepmother. Whenever I made a mistake she'd call me crazy or abnormal or accuse me of taking drugs. Maybe I was a little crazy, but I had never touched any drugs. I knew I couldn't handle them. I wasn't strong enough or brave enough to even try.

One thing I couldn't stand about my stepmother was

that she still saw my father. My father was living over in north London with his new girlfriend. I had no idea who she was. I'd never met her. Naturally, I would get upset when my stepmother visited him. I thought that she'd have a good laugh about me and agree with whatever my old perverted father said. If she noticed I was upset about her visits she would make cutting remarks like, 'I'm not the one with pictures of him all over the wall.' This sort of snide remark stung me. I only owned three pictures of my father – one of them was framed and I kept it on my chest of drawers. After that comment I removed it.

My stepmother wasn't all bad. She could be kind, intelligent and aware, but she's weak. After all, she stayed with a man who cheated on her and beat her so much that sometimes she didn't want to be seen in public because she was so battered. She even stayed with him when he beat her six-year-old son and punched his tooth right out of his mouth, and when he physically and sexually abused me, his nine- to eleven-year-old daughter.

Yet when I made 'mistakes' she was livid; like when I lost my virginity at the age of 14. She tried to keep me in the house, banned me from phone calls and called me a slag. I felt like a tramp and couldn't stand it.

I ran away to stay with a friend in north London and ended up in another children's home, where I still am now. My school friends helped to make me feel better once again and now I'm back on top of things and as ambitious as ever. I'm happy that at least I've managed to stay focused with my school work. In a way I've now decided it's time to move on.

Broken Promises

Emma Harris

My dad moved out before I was knee-high, before I could even pronounce his name properly. People seemed to assume that because I was young I didn't realise what was going on and that in a way I didn't need a father. I did, I still do! When my dad left, it hurt like hell!

There are times when I think how different my life could have been if certain things had never happened. If my mother had stayed with my father would I have been more courageous, witty or popular? The truth is, probably not. I'm me not because of my social class, my race or the people I live with, but because I was made this way.

To me it seemed like it was totally out of the blue, but I should have seen the signs – my dad's rages and my mum's tears. The final bust-up was the biggest and they battled it out for ages, all the hurt coming to the boil. Dad had been slamming every door in sight and Mum was slumped and crying on a kitchen chair. The tension that led up to it had been hovering over our house like a huge rain cloud. My mum had had enough of the constant arguing. She was upset, hurt and angry. She said she didn't love him any more, but I will never know if that was true. It was she who decided that it was in all our best interests if they split; my dad had a short temper and I don't think he and Mum ever really got along.

I didn't see my father for a while, and we settled down, just me and Mum. After a couple of months he decided he had the right to see me. And so began the unkept promises. Every so often he'd pop back into my life for an hour or two and then disappear again. Mum knew I was getting upset but she never put her foot down, never demanded that I shouldn't see him. I probably would have resented her if she had, but it might have made my life easier. I've always fitted in with Dad, always seen him when he turned up, but when I needed a father he was never there.

He's not really been a father to me, more a friend, and as I've grown older he's treated me as an adult. Because he's not been the authority figure that fathers normally are, I've felt like I could say anything to him and he doesn't give me a hard time – so he's good to talk to. He always takes me to see his friends when I go to visit him, and we usually go to the pub or play Nintendo. He still loves to show me off, but I can't help thinking that he doesn't deserve that right because he's not the one who's brought me up.

I remember Christmases when I'd wait up all night for him, waiting for him to bound in with the presents he'd promised me. Mum always said, 'He isn't going to come,' but I scowled through my teeth at her and hoped in vain. She was right and he rarely showed. My dad didn't realise how important he was to me. He didn't realise what his promises meant. After all, how can you tell a child that adults break promises? Yet, I always thought I was Daddy's little girl, I felt that way up until I was about 11. He said I was Daddy's little girl as he showed me off to his friends.

Once, when I was about five years old, I spent Christmas day with Dad, round at Nana's house. I'm really close to her and there were lots of relatives there, uncles, aunts, cousins and, of course, Grandad. Then I spent the evening round at my other nana's. Christmas was good that year, I had two big dinners and lots of presents. Even Dad gave me a present – I've only ever had about three presents from him in my life.

When I went to secondary school I met children who presumed I lived with my parents who had 2.4 children and a dog. When I told them I was an only child and my parents had split up, they wanted the gory details about how, where and why they weren't together any more. They weren't educated about why these things happen. I felt odd when teachers mentioned dads – I always thought that I'd missed out. I had to face the fact that my family wasn't the 'perfect' family that went on summer holidays together or ate together round a huge table. But I expected my parents to get back together in the end and I think my friends presumed they would because it seemed the 'right thing' for me.

The reunion never happened. When my dad started seeing other women it became more and more difficult for me to somehow invent a way in which my parents could get back together. I was always desperate to have brothers and sisters, so when I found out that one of my dad's girlfriends had a son by him but had had him adopted I tried searching for my half-brother. I didn't get anywhere.

I have mixed feelings about his current girlfriend – Tricia. At first I felt threatened by her, but she is nice and speaks to me like an adult; she's quite young herself and we really get on. I was excited when I heard she was pregnant for the first time and I was glad to see Dad happy. Together they've had three children, so at long last – I have a brother – Adam – and two sisters – Marcella and Sally. Without his girlfriend I wouldn't have them. The age gap is pretty big – there's five years between me and my oldest sister, but that doesn't seem to matter any more. I see them quite often and I love them as if they were my full brothers and sisters. When I go and visit I help Tricia to look after the kids. Then I go out with Dad to see his friends.

Dad's mad about karate and has loads of trophies. We're both interested in sports and I got into the martial arts when I was younger – judo, kickboxing and Tae Kwon Do. So we've got that in common, plus we both love drawing. And I inherited a stubborn streak from him.

When I was younger I always thought it was my fault that my parents split up, but how could it have been? All I did was exist. As a child you are taught how to eat properly, speak, brush your teeth and dress but never how to act or feel when your parents split up. So I learnt to cope in my own way. Then I started puberty and decided to rebel against everything my mother had ever taught me; it must have been a struggle for her to deal with on her own.

Now, as an older teenager, I can't say it doesn't bother me at all not having my father around but I don't think it has had a long-lasting effect on me. I have grown to accept that he will be there when he chooses and I now have plenty of friends who have grown up with only one parent or with remarried parents. I know it wasn't my fault that they broke up. It was meant to happen, and if they had stayed together for me, I would have been very unhappy because it would have been wrong for them. In a way, Mum is like a role model for me. She thought about me and she thought about herself. She had the strength to finish it even though she cared for him; she needed to carry on with her own life. There is this notion that children from broken homes (I hate this term) do not do well in life, and there will always be people who judge you on your background, but I am strong enough to stand on my own two feet and be living proof that people from 'broken homes' can do something with themselves.

A Two-Way Thing

Samantha Bradfield

I'm the oldest in our family. I've got a younger sister and two younger brothers. So when Dad told us he was leaving I felt I had to put on a brave face for the sake of the others. Of course there were tears. Mainly from my dad and my sister. My brothers were still too young to really take it in. I cried too, but probably more from the shock than anything. What was most upsetting was that Dad didn't give a reason for going at all. Apparently he wanted time and space to 'discover himself', which I suppose is understandable. He was abandoned as a baby and brought up in a white household, even though he is black. My mother is white, so he never really had the chance to explore his culture and heritage. Understandable, but still hurtful. I felt he was leaving us because we (especially me) did not look obviously mixed race or black. I thought that I wasn't enough of what he wanted.

Luckily, I had not really begun my selfish teenage phase so I was able to help out at home. My brothers and sister often got annoyed with me for telling them what to do and frequently stormed off shouting, 'You can't tell me what to do, you're not my mum!' Over the years that friction changed as we all grew used to the situation. We all have a very close relationship with my mother, who is very easygoing, and makes an effort to get on with our friends. Everyone at school was sympathetic about the separation, but I actually felt better because many of my friends had parents who had split up and I could now join in with their discussions. I was looking forward to being entitled to free school dinners!

We didn't really see that much of Dad. We started off staying with him every weekend, but then my sister and I began having other commitments and couldn't go as regularly. My brothers still went and stayed every other weekend, and my sister and I would join them for Sunday lunch and often a film. It was nice because we had this special time just for us. But this all changed when he met someone else. His new partner, Doreen, also has two children, a boy and a girl, of much the same age as my brothers. All of a sudden our private time was shared with these other children, which I didn't really appreciate. They transferred to the same school as my brothers, who also spent more time at the house, so they got to know one another. It's hard enough to put up with three younger siblings without having two more thrust on you!

Doreen is West Indian, and suddenly Dad started taking us to traditional African Kwanza celebrations (an alternative to Christmas and New Year), and to see black theatre groups. It was all very new and different to what I was used to, but very interesting. It would have been quite enjoyable had I not felt that I didn't really fit in with Dad's new life. This feeling increased at a community-organised Kwanza celebration in London. Walking through the door into the hall was very intimidating for me because I did not know what to expect. I also felt very paranoid, since I was being stared at as if I shouldn't be there. I sat around with my brothers and sister and we took part in a couple of quizzes, which was all right because I actually knew some of the answers! We were all enjoying it until I was tapped on the shoulder. I turned around to see the man who had organised the event, and he asked me to come with him for a quiet word. So I did. He asked me who I was here with, so I pointed at my dad and told him. He said that it was fine with him but that the performers who were due to come on were not going to because there was a white person in the audience. As you can imagine, my heart sank and I felt pretty upset. I went back to sit with my family and told them what the organiser had said. I wanted to cry, but when you are 15 and the oldest child it's just not the done thing! My dad and Doreen thought it was ridiculous and went to speak to the organiser again. The performers were still refusing to do the show and people were getting restless. The organiser was more than willing to throw the performers out for being so prejudiced, and Doreen wanted to stay. But my dad didn't want to make a fuss. So we had to leave. I was upset, but more than that, I was furious with my dad, although I didn't say anything. It felt as though he was embarrassed to stand up for me, and I felt not only isolated from that community but from my family and, more specifically, my dad. It was me they picked on, not anyone else. I was also irrationally angry with my youngest brother because it wasn't his fault we were asked to leave even though he has blond hair and paler skin than me! Which really wasn't fair of me.

It would almost have been fine if that had been the only incident that made me feel slightly unwanted. I remember one Christmas, Dad and Doreen threw a party at their house, to which we were all invited. It was okay, but as a teenager I didn't feel particularly comfortable socialising with adults. So I spent most of the evening entertaining the guests' children with my sister, where I was quite happy. My brothers were off on their own somewhere with Doreen's son, being teenage boys. Because I hadn't really been socialising, my dad and Doreen decided that they should have a series of dinner parties to introduce me to etiquette! (Luckily they soon dropped that idea!) I could have been viewed as moody and antisocial, but my behaviour was more because I felt uncomfortable and awkward in a strange new situation. Dad just didn't seem to understand that it was a completely different cultural experience for me, having been brought up in a very white and middle-class home. This was partly his fault, as he had never thought to introduce Afro-Caribbean culture to us before. Admittedly he hadn't introduced it to himself either! It was silly things as well, like the music. I have variously been described as an 'indie kid', a 'goth', and a 'dirty metaller(!)' by my brother, so a night full of reggae and swing is not exactly going to be my type of thing. If I can't jump around and headbang to it, I can't dance at all!

★

Unfortunately I don't really see that much of Dad now. This is partly because I am studying away from home. I don't see him that often even when I do go back home. We have drifted apart, especially since he and my mother went through quite an argumentative divorce. As I was the eldest, my mum used to talk things through with me, so I probably knew more than I needed to about the financial and legal arguments between my parents. This affected how I looked at my dad. I stopped seeing him as a parent (whom you love no matter what), and looked at him more as just a man who seemed to be making things hard for my mother.

I don't want to drift apart even further, and am trying to establish better contact with him. The problem is that he doesn't really talk about his feelings very much, and I seem to have inherited this trait from him! Obviously we have to work on our relationship, and at a different level than before. It is hard now I have my own life in a completely different city. He's always very busy with work. And for me, between working and studying and university life, staying in touch often falls by the wayside. It means we don't see that much of Dad's side of the family. My mum often won't be invited to weddings and things, so there are split loyalties. Visiting my nan is hard as my dad never tells me in advance when he will be going. This is what I feel most guilty about, as she is in a home and misses having people to talk to. She may not be my dad's real mother, but she is very special.

I know that relationships are a two-way thing, especially now I am counted as a grown-up, and I know that it is up to me as well as him to make an effort, but after so long I find it quite difficult. Ages ago we were told to think of his house as our home too, and to drop round whenever we wanted, but that is easier said than done when most of the time he is not likely to be in. It can be awkward sitting around waiting with people you don't really know in a strange house. I suppose if everything had been handled better in the first place it wouldn't seem so awkward, but as things are I shall just have to wait and see how it goes!

Look on the Bright Side

Cat Reilly

I guess you could say that I had a happy childhood. To me it seemed perfect, but then I didn't know any different. A big farmhouse in the middle of the countryside with fields to run around in and animals to play with. My parents took me on plenty of holidays to beautiful sunny countries. I still go on holidays, and I still live in a place that I love, but somehow it's not the same when there's only one parent.

This may not be the story as it happened exactly, the details may not all be correct, but that doesn't matter. It's how you remember it that counts.

I was about six and sitting in our cosy farmhouse kitchen when they told me, when the first blow hit. I thought this kind of thing only happened to other people.

There was a very uncomfortable atmosphere. I couldn't

help wondering what was going on and wishing that my feelings were wrong. My mum's usually soft features were hardened, she had bags under her eyes and worry lines on her forehead. Dad, on the other hand, just looked angry.

'Your mum's moving to London,' my father told me with an iciness in his voice that I'd never heard before. What? I don't get it. Why? What's wrong with here? My first thought was that it was my fault, that she didn't love me any more. She went on to give me details and endless apologies, but somehow all that didn't sink in too well. I didn't care, I just wanted us all to be together.

'Tell her the truth,' was my father's next sour remark.

'Well, love, I'm going to live with another woman.'

I didn't understand. So what? I thought, is there something odd about that? I didn't care where she was going or who with, I just cared that she wouldn't be with us. It wasn't until later that I realised this was slightly different from other families, it wasn't until the teasing started. But enough of that for the moment, let's get back to that day.

A sharp sigh from my father, and then the sobbing began. Never before had I seen either of them cry. It was a sight that I never expected but, then again, I'd never have expected my mum to leave either. I didn't quite know how to react. Here were these people that I'd always looked up to, the ones that I relied on when I was upset, doing the very thing that they comforted me for. I wondered if I should say something, and just as I was about to, the reality hit me. Why should I comfort them? It was me who was the victim here. So I joined in with the crying and didn't stop for a very long time. Even when the physical crying stopped, it took a long time for the small child inside of me to stop yelling out for all the things she'd lost.

So off she went, to London, leaving us hundreds of miles behind. I was told later that my mother had fought and lost a court case to keep me. For me there was no question of where I wanted to live. I didn't want to leave my wonderful house to live in a big, dirty city.

At first, she visited every second weekend. Each day we'd miss her more and more. I felt rejected, abandoned, as if she didn't love me any more. It was really hard; I was upset but at least I still had my mum to a certain extent. Dad had lost her for ever. He quickly became depressed, and I don't think he ever stopped being depressed, not until the day he died.

I don't remember much about the next few years, maybe that's because I just can't remember them, or maybe it's because I don't want to – who knows?

Every so often this woman would come round to visit our house and give me presents. Trying to win my love, I thought. Dad always said that he and she were just good friends. I may have been young, but I certainly wasn't stupid.

When Mum came to pick me up for the weekend she and Dad would usually have an argument about nothing in particular. After a while I'd go and scream at them to stop it, and run off crying. Then each of them would come and apologise. Note that they never came together, always one at a time, like they were ashamed to be seen together. The opposite effect to what I wanted. I used to hope that when they saw how unhappy I was they'd forget all the arguments and get back together. Of course

I knew that would never happen, but a little part of me liked to believe it. And who can really blame me?

Then there were the times I spent with my mother. I'd go and visit at 'their' flat in London. As far as my mum's partner went, I didn't like her and she didn't like me. I resented her for what she had done to my family, and she resented me for being my mum's first priority. We were both jealous of each other. Those weekends and holidays were pretty fraught, and all the time I was thinking of how lonely my dad would be all on his own. How he'd be drowning his sorrows with alcohol, which, of course, only made the depression worse, which in turn made him drink more. A vicious cycle. There was no way out. I noticed this but didn't like to say anything. He was so sensitive that I had to tread really carefully with what I said. I knew that if I put him down in any way, shape or form he'd think he was a useless father. He wasn't, he was the best father a girl could wish for. I knew that I was all he had left, the only thing that kept him going, that kept him waking up each morning.

When I was about 10, Mum moved back to the area, so I got to see her more. I also started secondary school in the town where she was living so I spent more time away from Dad. He got lonely, and I started blaming myself for him being 'fed up' as he called it. I now know that he suffered from clinical depression, but at the time I felt as if I was failing him as a daughter.

My dad had changed from being a fun-loving young person into an old man in a very short time. He was no longer the man that I'd known so well. It was hard to spend a lot of time with him. So the vicious circle continued and we grew apart. I was scared of the different man that stood before me. I still loved him like mad but he was not the same. I always knew that he was older than most dads, 59 when I was born, and I also knew, even though I didn't like to admit it to myself, that he would most likely die before I was properly grown up. Knowing that didn't make it any easier when it happened. When he died I was distraught. He was 72 and I was 13. I felt the little girl rise back to the surface and begin to scream again.

Now I live with Mum and her new partner, who I get on really well with. She's a youth worker and I have been involved with some of the drama projects that she has organised. This has helped me to get to know her separately, without my mum as a bridge. We have a different kind of relationship to that which you would have with anyone else. I don't see her as a parent figure because she's not, but I do feel she is a friend I can talk to any time I need that extra bit of support. We are very close in our own way. The fact that she is a woman helps me to relate to her; to me a man in the house would give me constant reminders of my father, which I wouldn't be able to cope with.

None of my friends have a problem with my mum being a lesbian. They get on so well with her that sometimes I think they come over to see her, not me!

When I first started secondary school I got a bit of stick from the older boys, but when they realised that it didn't get to me, they gave up. Some of them still have a problem and I get pointless remarks thrown at me now and again but I don't care what they think, it's what I think that counts.

It's four years since my dad died and over 11 since my parents split up. It's a long time, but over the last couple of years I've become a much more positive person, and although the angry little girl surfaces once in a while, I don't let her take over my life. I enjoy school and have a good time with my friends. The bad memories will never go away but I've learnt to deal with them and get on with my life as best I can.

The Man of the House and his Tribe of Little Sisters

Stephanie Fowler

My brother and sister and I are very good friends, despite (or because of) being siblings, and they are the two people I can always confide in. Ten years after our parents' divorce, we do occasionally talk about it, but I can still recall one conversation which took place between my brother and me a long time ago. He was being very reasonable, considering that I was whining in true Judy Blume/*Sweet Valley High* style. By this time, Dad had moved up to Scotland, but still came down a couple of times each year to stay at our nan's, whose house is about 10 minutes away. I was complaining that when he came to visit with my stepmother and half-sister, I didn't feel like he was my father, just a friend with his family. Then, having just read *Nineteen Eighty-four* (where the main character is tortured and betrays the woman he loves), I said I didn't know whether I loved him or not.

My brother said, 'Of course you do.'

'No,' I said, 'I don't.'

'Yes you do.'

'Why?'

'Because he's your dad.'

I always felt my brother seemed to have no problems about Dad not living with us any more. As far as I remember, either he coped exceptionally well during the divorce, or he didn't appear to react at all. Obviously, it's easier to remember how I dealt with it; like being amazed at the tricks my mind could play, and at the connection my mum and the teachers made between the divorce and how often I was absent or sent home from school. When I started secondary school, I probably spent about half the time at home, because I was always waking up feeling ill. But by the end of the first year, the school gave me an achievement award for improvement.

Back at nursery and primary school, even though my brother's a year older than me, we were sometimes put in the same class. I remember my mum saying that one teacher had remarked that she'd rarely seen a sister and brother who were such good friends. The only time the two of us didn't get on particularly well was in secondary school, just after the divorce. All three of us (my brother, sister and me) and our mum stick together. Today we are one of the closest families I know.

So there he was, 'the man of the house', a phrase which became a joke, especially whenever he wanted to get his own way (bellowing, 'But I'm the man of the house!'). But I could forgive his petty use of the term in arguments, after all, I helped put that label on him. And it's strange, some of the jokes we made; for example, my dad's name is Michael, and after he left, my brother looked at one of the Christmas cards we'd received, and said, 'They've taken the mickey out of our family.'

Like all children, we used to think about the future. We'd draw plans of the huge homes we'd acquire, think up names for our children and, as we'd never travelled further than Wales, decide where in America we would live (I was sent to Canada at one point). I was exceptionally fervent about my future children; adamant that I would have at least one girl, and that no matter what, my first child must be a boy. I only recently realised this was because I didn't believe that marriage would be for ever, so I desperately wanted my daughters to have a father figure in their older brother. I now think I wouldn't mind if I did have a girl first.

Dad leaving has definitely meant I've treated my brother differently, and this isn't really fair on him. I cringe when I think of our worst arguments and what I say when I've run out of steam and insults. He tells me to be on my way, so as I flourish off on my grand exit, I spit the legend, 'Yes, Dad!' Afterwards we laugh at this because it is so very sick, after all.

While wrapped up in my expectations of him, as big brother and father figure, I didn't realise that he had his own particular problems – as the eldest, understanding better what had happened, and as a boy growing up without his father, in a house full of women. I eventually found out what was hardest for him was thinking he should have stopped our parents getting divorced, although he knew that wouldn't have been the best thing to do, because we are happy as we are. He sorted his problems out in his own way, and for some time now, he and my dad have found common ground in the pub, alcohol and cigarettes. He hasn't missed out not having a father, and their friendship is something they're comfortable and happy with.

As the oldest daughter, I have a different relationship with my dad, because I can't go to the pub with him and chat up the barmaid. I realised I had to figure something out for myself, a way to get on with him, and to put the past in the past. This was more than achieved when I recently discovered the virtues of football.

Like my brother, I know that when my parents split up 10 years ago, they stopped being husband and wife, but they never stopped being Mum and Dad. However, there was still someone in our family who hasn't yet come to terms with the divorce.

For such a communicative lot it's amazing what can suddenly crop up after all these years. One of my main hobbies is writing, and I recently finished a story about divorce, which ends with the news being broken to the youngest child, who then asks her older sister, 'What does "divorce" mean?' Coincidentally, I found out that my own sister had been in a similar predicament as the baby sister who didn't understand. We then discovered that she hadn't even known that the divorce was because our dad had had an affair with our stepmother. One thing that made me feel worse was that my friend who was there at the time knew about it, but my sister didn't. We'd all of us taken it for granted that she must have known what was happening.

I do remember we all dealt incredibly well with the announcement about our new half-sister. We were excited about her arrival, not jealous, and love her as if she were our real sister. In fact, everyone remarks how much she looks like my sister. I can understand that our half-sister must feel confused at times, because there have been awkward questions in the past, like the time she said, 'My dad is your dad, but my mum isn't your mum. So where's your mum?' It must have sounded strange when we told her our mum was at home. As she has grown up, she has been taught to call us her brother and sisters, and has had no problem with this, but I wonder when there'll be some more explaining to do. As my mum recently pointed out, our half-sister is now seven, the same age as my sister was when our parents split up.

The arrival of the new baby last year, another girl, probably caused more problems for our little sister than it did for us. She asked what would happen to her once the new baby arrived, and she must have thought that she would no longer get the attention she always received as the youngest of four children. Of course, when Dad remarried and our first half-sister was born, my sister had to face similar problems. Now, however, my biggest problem has nothing to do with the divorce – my dad's new family live so far away that I can only see my one-year-old sister sporadically.

The latest conversation with my brother focused on our two half-sisters. We shot through the usual what-would-have-beens, because we are aware that we'll never know what life would be like now, if our parents had stayed together.

I have always considered the situation like this: if Dad had stayed, would I have gone to a festival last year, or would my sister and I have gone to nightclubs from the ages of 14 and 16, and, above all, would I have had my eyebrow pierced, and she her belly button? Of course, Dad knows all about these things that we get up to, but perhaps feels he cannot do much to stop them happening. So in turn, he's a cooler dad, not allowing us to get away with murder, but accepting and maybe respecting our decisions and being cool about the way Mum has brought us up.

Funnily enough, what helped create some common ground between me and my dad – football – is the very thing which helped me establish that my brother is my brother rather than a father figure. I nagged him for ages and ages to take me to a match and we now go regularly. It's not a question of him taking me (like a parent), but the two of us go together. And we certainly behave like typical siblings – fighting like cat and dog about who gets the better seat.

I do know that the way things turned out, I wouldn't change the situation – my brother and all my little sisters – for anything.

Not the End of the World

Sarah Fowler

I was only eight when my parents got divorced so I didn't really understand what this meant exactly. The way I saw it, it was like an adventure to go on trips to my dad's for dinner and to walk in the local park in West Kirby. All I understood was everyone was making a fuss of me as I was the youngest, but I enjoyed the attention instead of understanding what was happening. I met my step-mother Debbie shortly after the divorce. I thought she was great then because she went out on a limb to get on with us – buying us things, making us nice things for dinner. Although I remember worrying about my mum, she seemed to be coping fine.

Less than a year later, in the following May, my dad and my stepmum got married near Glasgow – they married in Scotland because of Debbie's relatives. It was another adventure to me, especially as me and my brother and sister stayed in a hotel with my nan. I remember the wedding really clearly – all Dad's friends looked after us and Debbie's friends and relatives made a fuss of us. Our step-grandad was very wealthy and we'd spend lots of time in his huge house.

After the wedding, my dad and Debbie lived nearby and we'd see them about twice a week. For a while me and Debbie were getting on really well, doing their grocery shopping and such like together. We probably got on so well then because I was the youngest and didn't see anyone as an enemy.

I don't think they were married too long before Debbie fell pregnant with my baby sister Rosie, which coincidentally marks my first bad memory of her. I made her a congratulations card and all she did was point out that I'd spelt pregnancy wrong. I couldn't understand why she was being nasty as she'd never seemed fussy before. However, we were all over the moon. Debbie bought a pregnancy book and every week we'd look at it together and work out how big the baby would be.

I suppose in a way things went down hill from then on, except that I had the most beautiful little sister (the day Rosie was born we were told by Dad to call her our sister not our stepsister). Debbie spent less time with us and seemed more interested in Rosie. Now I can see that she had just had her first child with the man she loved, but at 11 or 12 I just felt upset.

When Rosie was about six months old, Dad lost his job making furniture because our family firm folded. The business had been set up by my great-grandfather. All his sons had worked there and most of their sons, so most of my family suffered from its collapse. Debbie's father got

Dad a very different job in a post office and general store in a quiet part of Scotland, so they had to move. We live in Merseyside, so it is about five hours on the train to where they live. I was sad to lose them all but I think I was most upset about missing out on Rosie's growing up, as she was changing so much at the time.

When they first moved, Dad would pay for our tickets to visit and while they worked we'd sit in the back of the post office and play around. We'd always do nice things like go shopping in Edinburgh, but we dreaded going to visit Debbie's elderly granny who owned a farm in Strathclyde. She was really sweet, but we'd stay for dinner and have to eat the most dreadful food! She'd make us sloppy meat and vegetables – it was so awful you couldn't recognise anything. Dad would get annoyed if we didn't make a good effort to eat most of it; he wanted to get on well with Debbie's relatives and didn't want us to seem rude.

Rosie is still one of the most amazing kids I know. She is so full of energy and spends hours running around urging us to join in with her. I think she's the only kid I know who can spend all day travelling and still play in the park for hours. Dad phones us once a week and she always talks too, telling us about her friends and school. It's sometimes weird as she has such a strong Scottish accent I can't always understand her. I have to ask her to repeat herself and then she gets in a mood.

I remember when Rosie was old enough to begin to understand. I was with her one afternoon and she asked, if I was her sister how come we don't have the same mum. That took some explaining. She once went through a big possessive stage and told me and my sister that our dad was only her dad. When I asked how come, she said because Dad lives with her and not us. That took some explaining, too.

One of Rosie's bad points is that she has the worst temper I've ever seen on a child. If we won't do something she wants to do – like play a certain game or something – she'll sulk and say, 'I hate you', then giggle to try to convince us to do whatever she wants again. She's a sweet girl though, she's very affectionate and a great little sister. I do feel bad that I can't visit her as much now. I had thought I might start writing to her as she's getting good at writing. My sister and I thought the next time she comes to visit us we'll take her out for the day, to the pictures or something, so we can spend more time with her.

When Rosie was five, my baby sister Louise was born. I couldn't go up to visit for a while around that time so I didn't even see her till she was a few months old. I've only got one photo of her – I've a million of Rosie from when she lived locally. I've still only seen Louise a few times. It does upset me that she probably has no idea about me and my brother and sister as she sees so little of us. I doubt anyone sits down and explains to her who we are and we'll completely miss out on her growing up. I guess the only thing I can do is try to visit more often. I know Rosie understands who we are because we were around her so much when she was younger, but sometimes I think we've missed out on that kind of bond with Louise.

My dad and Debbie come down here to visit us more now that Louise's a bit older, but their visits always seem the same. Debbie sits and talks to my nan, and my dad and sisters sit in the front room with us. I almost feel that Debbie thinks she doesn't have to bother socialising with us now she has her own kids. I do want to make a conscious effort to get on better with Debbie, but she can seem awfully funny with us. When I was seventeen, I was sitting with my twenty-one-year-old brother and twenty-year-old sister, and my stepmother left the room we were in with our half-sisters. Debbie turned to Rosie and told her to keep an eye on the baby. Maybe she wasn't thinking but it was as if she didn't trust us with her baby.

I sometimes feel that my dad doesn't know me too well either. When I said I'd visit him one morning before he left he said he'd take a picture of me in my school uniform. I smiled and reminded him that I hadn't been in school for two years since I started college – and since I was taking my A levels we were on study leave anyway. However, it probably just slipped his mind.

Sometimes my friends will ask me if I ever wish my parents were back together. I have to smile and reply with an emphatic no. Initially, this was all I'd dream of (literally), but if they'd never split up I wouldn't have my little sisters or excuses to go to Scotland for quick holiday breaks. I guess it took a long time for me to understand that divorce is a good thing if people don't love each other any more. My dad is happy with his new family, and my mum is a lot happier now, too, so I think things eventually worked out for the best.

Chloe's Life Story

Chloe Johnson

Up until I was five, I assume I had an average family. It was me, my younger sister Tanya, my dad, and my mum. How more normal could you get? But one day, after a fantastic holiday at my nanan's, something happened that I was totally unprepared for.

My nanan lives in Wales. My dad didn't go with us on that holiday but I was too little to think that anything was strange about that. Then Dad was there to meet us off the train when we returned. Mum said, 'Your dad's going to take you home and then he's going to go away for a while.'

I can't believe now that I just carried on as if nothing had happened. It all seemed perfectly normal at the time. Me and Tanya and Mum carried on living in our house at Cobham Road. Every other weekend, we went to visit our dad, who was staying with friends. I remember they had a gorgeous dog called Becky! Now, my dad has his own house where we still go every other weekend.

After about two years, my mum met a man called Mark. They decided that we should live together. This was a problem since Mark and his three sons lived in Bedford and we lived in Sheffield. After a lot of discussion, it was decided that Mark and his sons would move here, but only after we had visited Bedford. I can only say that I did not like it there. Especially as I spent my first night without a light on all night (scary!). We had another problem, too. The house that Mum, me and my sister shared was too small to fit the two families together, so guess what? We had to move anyway. That was exciting, but very sad for me because I really missed our big garden and cosy little house. I can even remember the biscuit cupboard though it's something like six years since I last sneaked in it for a snack!

Back to the move – it was actually really good fun, especially the moving van. I remember it well because it had a little platform at the back that moved up and down and I loved standing on it. Me and Mum and my sister stayed in our new house by ourselves for a couple of weeks before Mark and his boys moved in. At first, Mark scared me a bit because he was so different to my dad. But he was an excellent storyteller and I can remember me and Tanya and his youngest son Steve snuggled up around Steve's bed listening to *The Lord of The Rings*, or some funny or mysterious poem (our favourite was 'The Frying Pan in the Moving Van').

At first, I was shy of my new stepbrothers and I didn't know how to behave around them. I think I liked living with them, but my friends went on about it and that got a bit annoying! I sometimes got jealous – I thought my stepbrothers were giving more attention to my sister than me. I was really protective towards her, but after a while I got used to it and then everything became really nice. We had lots more games and a lot of fun together. It was great not being the eldest any more. In the park, Mark's sons (Steve, Geoff and Nick) would take it in turns to give the two of us piggybacks. Having older brothers meant that I had someone to give me piggybacks and play games with, as well as a little sister who I could do the same to.

One hard thing about the two families coming together was that we were all so different, especially with food. We were used to white bread, chocolate bars and crisps, but Mark made his own bread and his family ate a lot of healthy food that Tanya and I thought was disgusting at first! In the end, we made a compromise. We still had to get used to Mark's home-made bread – but I can't tell the difference now. Another thing was that Mark, Steve, Geoff and Nick all ate meat whereas Mum, Tanya and I are all vegetarians and detest the idea of eating animals. Mark gave up meat altogether and the boys only eat meat at Christmas or at their Mum's.

Christmas itself caused problems. Tanya and I soon found that the boys were not going to let us put baubles just anywhere on the tree. Oh no, they had a system, which meant that we weren't allowed anywhere near it! Also, Mark and his sons always went to church on Christmas Day (we had never been before). Imagine our faces after we had opened our stocking presents and run downstairs to start ripping the paper off our big presents only to find we had to go to church first!

Then Mum and Mark decided to get married. I wasn't sure about it but after a while I thought, this is quite good, it's bringing us more together. At the Registry Office, as Mum and Mark were saying the words for the marriage, it was as if the whole family was becoming really close. At the same time, I was feeling a bit guilty, as if Tanya and I were getting further apart from our dad. I think the boys must have been feeling a bit like that too, about their mum. I could see my dad didn't really mind, so it doesn't bother me any more. To begin with I wasn't sure about changing to Mark's surname, but I thought it would be stupid to have a different name from Mum and it's really good because now I'm higher up on the register at school!

I've always been very active and achieved a lot. I'm good at art and music and I have loads of friends at school, but I do get jealous of my friends because I think they've got a normal life – just a mum and a dad. In a way, it's a bit weird having two families and I'm still wondering what my life would have been like if it was still just my mum, my dad, Tanya and me.

Looking back to when my mum and my dad were still together, I think that it wouldn't have worked out if Dad had stayed. They were always arguing. I didn't know what to think then, but now I can see how very different they were. Just like heaven and hell, total opposites! I'm just glad that my life's really good and that I've got really nice families. When I see or hear about kids who have got messed up because of a divorce, I feel really sorry for them.

★

One evening, Mum said, 'How would you lot feel if I said I was going to have a baby?' I couldn't believe it, I was amazed. Everything was going to be brilliant, except that Mum had a very bad pregnancy and threw up all over the place! She also had a mad craving for Polo mints. After finding out that Mark had put six packets of Polos on top of a very tall cupboard, she climbed up on a chair – eight months pregnant – and guzzled every one! Hope was born in hospital, although she was intended to be born at home. Mum had been in labour the night before and was carted off to hospital in an ambulance because she was having trouble giving birth.

I remember waking up in the morning after Hope's birth and rushing downstairs yelling, 'Is it a boy or a girl – tell me, tell me?' And Mark, exasperated, had to tell me and my sister a hundred times that Mum had had a baby girl. I went into the hospital room and saw this tiny, little, scrunched-up face, covered in dark hair. She was so cute! I thought I was so lucky. I remember holding her. She was so delicate, I was terrified of dropping her. I immediately fell in love with her.

Just before Hope was born, Steve, Tanya and I played games in which, if you lost one game, you would have to change the baby's first wet nappy, and if you lost two games you would have to change the baby's first yucky nappy! It ended up with me losing one game and Steve losing two. He was horrified. He dreaded even being in the same room when Hope was having her nappy changed!

I think Hope brought the two families together even more – if Mum and Mark took her for a walk, we'd all go along and want to play with her. We'd end up having a brilliant time. At first, I was a tiny bit jealous of Hope – I thought, oh no, another new person in the family – but it's impossible not to like her, we get on really well.

Because there's so many other people in the family, I don't get as much attention as I'd like and that can be a bit tricky. But going to my dad's helps because I get loads and loads of attention from him all the time. It's really nice. I visit my dad every other weekend and we do things like climbing, walking and swimming. We try to pack in as much as we can. I like going to Dad's just as much as being at Mum's, except that he annoys us sometimes because he's always spoiling us.

I've got so used to my separate families that we all seem to be like one big family in which we love one another very much. I wouldn't change my family for the world; no, make that the universe!

C'est la Vie

Harriet Flynt

Mum is always telling me how hard it is being a single parent and how I don't help her enough. To some extent, I suppose I don't. I'm just your average teenager. When I'm not at school I like to laze around the house, watching television and listening to music. I never really appreciate the hell she has to go through, working as a full-time teacher and looking after three teenage children. I don't think I could do it, and I think that my mum is very brave. However, I do know what the pain is like living without my dad.

My dad left seven years ago when I was ten years old. As every young child would be, I was devastated. He had been having an affair and moved two hours' journey away. I didn't understand why he had left and asked my mum for days why – and why he didn't love me enough to stay at home. It was a violent shock to my family – my

75

two older brothers, Craig and Robert, and my mum. Our lives were changed in unimaginable ways. No one knows what it feels like to have your dad leave home unless it has happened to them. It's one of the worst things that can happen to you and I know that it totally wrecked my childhood. I think it must be even worse if your mum leaves, and I'm very grateful that that wasn't the case for me. Everyone tells me that I should have got over it by now, but I know that I never will. I was lucky. I never got beaten up, my parents rarely argued in front of me, I was never abused. In fact, I had two wonderful parents, which made it more of a shock. I thought everything was fine. No one told me anything until the day it happened. I know I have a lot of anger bottled up inside me that won't come out for years and years to come.

I would say that I am a completely different person to who I would have been if my dad was around now. I don't know if that is a good or bad thing really. I've had a hard knock, self-confidence wise, and I'm always worrying about what people think of me and whether they genuinely like me. My two best friends are Marnie and Ruth. I met them when I started secondary school, two years after my dad left, and they have been superb. They are wonderful people. They are always there for me whenever I need them. If I am ever feeling upset about anything, I know that I can just ring them and they will help me sort it out. They have really helped me build my confidence up. Sometimes I feel that they don't understand, because they both come from two-parent families. I get worried in case they think I moan too much. I even get worried that they don't like me sometimes but, of course, that is never true. They are two wonderful friends and I am glad to have them.

I also grab on to things for support. I use other things to cement the gap that was made when my dad left. At thirteen, I had an intense passion for the pop group Boyzone. It turned everyone in my home insane. I played their music all the time, I covered my walls with their pictures and I would spend endless amounts of money on their merchandise. It was ridiculous and, when I think back, quite scary. I still like them now, but not to the same extreme, thank goodness. I know that people who lead normal, stable lives with two parents get obsessed like that as well, but I'm not the sort of person to behave like that. I needed something that would replace the father figure image. I also became very attached to the film *Titanic*. I absolutely adored it. I went to see it seven times at the cinema and bought all the CDs, books and posters. My dad would ring and ask me why I liked it so much. I couldn't tell him that it was his fault. Both Boyzone and *Titanic* made me happy and seemed to fill the gap that my dad's leaving had made.

One thing I am grateful for is that I can have a good relationship with my dad now, which I know a lot of people can't do. It was about six months until I even spoke to my dad after he left. I was so angry and bitter towards him that I didn't want to talk to him. I was even afraid of him because I thought he would tell me things I didn't want to hear, like, 'You're going to be coming to live with me.' Things did get better, and Dad started to come and visit my family. Him and Mum became sort of friends, and when he came it was like it had always been, although I could never imagine living with my dad now.

I used to cry when his visit ended because I didn't want him to leave. He always seemed so lovely and nice, but Mum said that I had to think what he would be like if he lived with us. He would be horrible and get cross. Maybe that's true, but it doesn't stop me from being sad about him even now. When he comes to see us, I can feel the tension in Mum. They often have rows and it really upsets me. Mum says that when I eventually leave home she will have nothing more to do with him. As for me, I have a much better relationship with my dad than I would have if he was still living with us. We talk on the phone every week and he writes to me. We go on holiday together about twice a year. I even think he's a nice and funny person! I'm glad that I can love him so much after everything that has happened in our family.

Going on holiday with my dad is something that I enjoy immensely. Because I liked Boyzone, I asked him to take me to Ireland last year and we went again this year. We are planning to go to Dublin next year. I love spending time with him, just chatting about everyday things and enjoying the scenery together. Ireland is a beautiful place. I like looking at the scenery, and my dad studies stone circles, a great passion of his. This means that we can both go somewhere together and enjoy ourselves and our different interests at the same time. It's not something every family, split up or otherwise, gets the chance to do.

However, he doesn't know me very well and that makes me sad. When I was taking my GCSEs, he thought I was taking only two exams, maths and English, until the summer when I took all nine and a half of them. He hadn't even asked me what I was doing. It might be that he is forgetful or that he can be quite selfish sometimes. He often goes on holiday abroad and usually only tells me he is going about two weeks beforehand. I just wish that he cared a lot more about what I'm doing.

I've also had problems with his girlfriend. I would call her his girlfriend, but she's too old; perhaps lady-friend is better. For ages I hated her. I'd never met her and, frankly, I didn't want to. I felt that she made my dad leave and divorce my mum, and I directed a lot of my anger towards her. When my dad first left, I used to think that she had hypnotised him because she works as a hypno-therapist. I think that's quite unlikely now, but you never know! I don't know whether I've felt all this because I am so angry with her or whether I am worried about what Mum will think. Mum doesn't want me to meet my dad's woman because she is worried that she will take her place, which is ridiculous, of course, but I can't blame my mum for that.

There's one incident that happened when I began to ring my dad quite regularly. Before, I had been too scared to ring in case his girlfriend answered and I didn't want to speak to her. Well, one time she answered and I hadn't planned what I was going to say to her and I was scared stiff. I said, 'Um, is Steve Flynt there, please?' She asked who was calling and in my panic I answered, 'Oh, um, um, Doris!' She instantly knew that it was me, rather annoyingly. Even worse, she told Craig, my brother, about it every time he stayed there. I didn't like the fact that she talked about me and I never wanted to see her. But then, not long ago, I finally agreed to meet her.

I felt it was time to face up to the fact that my dad was with someone else, and that he was happy. The meeting was an ordeal but I am glad that I went through with it. I know Mary is not the dragon that I had pictured her to be. She tries so hard to get along with me that I think it's easier to accept her as a part of my dad's life. Hopefully, this is the start of a new relationship with my dad and things will get better for us.

My dad has moved pretty far away from us, to Taunton, in Somerset. This means that I don't get to see him very often, about once a month. My mum, brother and I live in a town in Bedfordshire, having moved here two years ago. We used to live in a huge house in a little village. It was two cottages knocked together that my dad was doing up. It was unfinished when he left. For three people a five-bedroomed house felt a little vast, so we eventually moved to our current house. It is a wonderful three-bedroomed cottage and there is nothing that I would change about it – apart from the attitudes of the people who live around here. It is a very aristocratic and wealthy area. I don't think the people take too kindly to single-parent families. In the two years that we've been here we have seen our neighbours about twice. I think they may be embarrassed because they don't understand how we feel. It doesn't bother me, but it does bother my mum a little – she would like to know some more people where we live.

My mum has had it pretty bad. I've tried to understand what she feels but, especially after all these years, she manages to hide it away. I would love her to find another boyfriend, so I could have another sort of dad and so she could be happy, but I know she never will. She doesn't want one and I think she's too scared in case she gets rejected again. It does get hard because we fight a lot, but hopefully that's just my adolescent stage and I'll grow out of it. I love her very much and will always be around for her whenever she needs me.

It's going to take time for me to forgive my dad, but now I'm 17 I feel I am slightly more mature and able to deal with the situation. Although this has happened to me, I couldn't be happier now. It's not something that I get upset about every day and I can manage to get on with my life without thinking about it all the time. I love both my parents very much, and though one of them lives far away, I'm glad that they are both alive and love me too.

Cold Chicken

Melanie O'Brien

My mum and dad split up a long time ago, so really it's all I've ever known and I don't mind it. I suppose that makes me lucky, but there are still problems. I only see my dad one weekend every fortnight, and my mum and my dad still row sometimes.

One of the worst times was when Mum was really upset with Dad about something, I don't know what. She stormed about the house for a bit, then phoned him and said, 'I just want you to know I hate you and I don't want you in my house any more!'

My twin brother and I both heard Mum say it. My older sister came down a bit later and heard Mum shouting about it. Then my brother and sister both went upstairs. Our supper was on the table: roast chicken with roast potatoes, it's usually one of my favourite meals. I just sat for a while in the living room. Then I washed my hands and sat at the dinner table. I know it seems like a really stupid thing to do, but I was dazed, I didn't think about what I was doing.

After what seemed like ages I realised there was no way we were going to eat any time soon, and I was starting to feel dumb sitting there by myself. My brother and sister were upstairs; I can't remember where my mum was. So I went upstairs, I didn't particularly want to see them right then, but I didn't know what else to do.

They were both in the room that I share with my sister, crying. My brother kept saying, 'We'll never see Dad again, we'll never see Dad again.' Over and over again. My sister said nothing, she just cried. And I sat there doing nothing at all. I know that makes me seem really cold, but I'm not, I just express my feelings in a different way, or not at all. I know I should express myself more, but I won't force myself to cry, there's no point. I tried to see how we could go on seeing Dad, but every possibility seemed more impossible than the last.

After we had calmed down a bit we all went down-stairs and sat at the dinner table. We sat there in silence while Mum served us. She kept saying things like, 'Of course, your dad has ruined dinner.'

I hate that, why can't they just call each other by their first names? Dad's the same. It's like he's forgotten what Mum's name is, or he's talking about someone he's never met before. I wondered what my dad was doing at that moment. I wondered if he was as upset as me, and what he was thinking.

Anyway, we sat there brooding. Then my brother mouthed the words we'd all been wanting to say, 'Mum, will we ever see Dad again?'

Mum sort of smiled and said, 'Of course, darling, everything will be the same as before, he just won't come into the house any more.'

I suddenly realised how tense I'd been, as I felt a wave of calm wash over me. My brother started crying again, I guess it was in relief. I just sat there chewing my now cold chicken.

For a while, things were difficult. Mum tensed up if she picked up the phone and it was Dad. Messages had to pass from Dad through us to Mum, and then back through us to Dad. Then, after a while they started speaking to each other, Dad came inside when he picked us up and dropped us off, Mum started laughing at his jokes again, and he came to our house last Christmas. Things are as good as they can be now, with my parents living apart.

You often read stories or hear about people who hate their mum's or their dad's boyfriend/girlfriend, but I've never experienced that. My dad's got a girlfriend right now and I think she's great, we really get along and she makes me laugh. She's also got a daughter who's my age and a son who's three. I'm really good friends with her daughter, and the son is quite cute.

My mum does have a big problem with Dad's girlfriend though. After I'd stayed round at her house for the night, Mum refused to let her drop me off, it had to be my dad who took me home. While I was staying over at my dad's girlfriend's house, she started to tell me how immature my mum was being. I felt myself boiling with rage; how dare she insult my mum! But really it doesn't matter what she thinks. I love my mum, it's as simple as that.

For a while, things were really awkward with my dad and his girlfriend, Tania. We were staying at my dad's house for the whole of half-term, which I was really happy about as it meant I could spend some proper time with him. But when I got there Dad spoke really quietly, and when we got inside he went straight to the phone and started talking down it angrily. He was on the phone for ages, then when he came off, he looked as if he was about to cry.

After a while, he said, 'I'm really sorry about this, kids, but Tania isn't too happy with me right now. She's annoyed because I'm spending the whole weekend with you guys and not her. She says it means the only time she'll get to see me is after work, and by then I'm really tired. She thinks I care more about you lot than I do about her, she's really angry and I think she's right.'

I was outraged, of course he should care more about us, we're his children! And for him to think he shouldn't is ridiculous. I just hope I misunderstood what he meant. For the rest of that week, Dad seemed a bit preoccupied, and he kept having quiet phone calls with his girlfriend. I couldn't wait for the week to end. But despite all this, I still really like Dad's girlfriend – I can't help it, she's just likeable.

I used to wish that my mum and dad would get back together. That Dad would move back in and we would all be happy again. But now I realise it's not as simple as that. I would have been twice as miserable as I am now (not that I'm miserable). There would be constant arguments, or at least long silences. Mum said that was the worst thing, they didn't have great blazing rows, but they had long silences when they wouldn't talk to each other.

When Dad first moved out, he stayed at a friend's house, and then he moved to this house in Oxford. It was quite nice, but Oxford was such a long way away. Then Dad moved to a flat in Oxford – I didn't like it there, there was no central heating and there was only one bedroom. Now he's bought a flat that's much nearer to home – you can get there in a short bus ride, which makes life much easier.

One of the best things about my dad now is that he makes us talk when things are upsetting us. He sits us all down at the table and we pass an object round (like a glove or a pen – it doesn't matter what it is), and we can only talk if we're holding it. I always dread it beforehand; sometimes we row, sometimes I cry, sometimes my dad cries, but we always feel better for having got things off our chests, and afterwards there's a much more relaxed atmosphere around the flat.

I know it's not that uncommon any more for parents to split up, lots of my friends' parents have split up too. There are loads of stories about families breaking up, but I have never read stories that are at all similar to what's happened in my family. Maybe authors think my type of story is boring, that people don't want to read about parents that have the odd problem but can still talk civilly to each other. But it is still difficult for the people involved, especially the children.

Smile

Ruby Khan

People think of me as very bright and cheerful. That's because I go round with a smile on my face. I usually hide my feelings and sometimes lie to please others so that they think everything is okay. Like when my parents divorced I didn't tell my friends and I didn't show the world what I was going through. In reality everything changed. Isn't it strange how just one decision that isn't even yours can destroy everything? Your dreams, your family. I even found it hard to smile for a while.

I have always felt sorry for kids whose parents are divorced or separated. The parents both go their separate ways while the kids are left to choose ·between them. I believe that when a man and a woman get married they should stay together through thick and thin. If not for themselves, then for the sake of their children. The parents can go away and find new partners, but the children can't. Divorce affects the children more than the parents.

The date of my parents' divorce was 15 November 1997. My dad had been getting more and more moody, and in the end it was Mum who asked for the divorce. I didn't blame her and in a way I wasn't surprised, although I wasn't at all ready for it. I was eleven when it happened and I cried every night until my twelfth birthday. Mum couldn't really help me, she was busy trying to find some relatives who would let us stay with them. Dad had moved out and she was worried about not having a man around the house. She was scared of burglars and so was I.

My twelfth birthday came so slowly it was more like my forty-eighth! I've always loved my birthdays – I get such wonderful gifts – and I remember thinking that my birthday would make me feel better. But it didn't. Dad told us that he was remarrying and that we would have a stepmother, two stepsisters (twins), and a stepbrother. He thought I would be happy because I'd have another family, and he thought I'd like to have a brother. So far, in my family I had three sisters: the eldest was then aged eighteen, and the two little ones were aged three and one-and-a-half. But it was just another one of my beliefs down the drain. I believed that you should only marry once. Why were all the things I believed in being proved wrong?

Dad begged me to go to his wedding, but I was so angry I refused. My sisters, cousins, aunts and uncles went. Being angry with Dad wasn't the only reason why I didn't go. To tell you the truth, I didn't want to leave my mum on her own. I've always been like that, looking out for people.

When my sisters came back from the wedding they were so excited they couldn't stop talking about my dad's new wife, Sameera, and her kids. From the way they were talking I knew they would be moving in with my dad and Sameera. I wasn't so sure about my youngest sister but then she started calling Sameera mummy. My sisters have always been closest to my dad. He's kind and cracks loads of jokes, whereas my mum is more serious. To tell you the truth, I'd rather have lived with my dad, but I felt responsible for my mum. The divorce was her idea but I could see she was really upset. I thought I could comfort her by staying with her.

I think at that time I was pretty jealous of my dad and his new family. There were eight of them and only two of us. The thought of my dad being with another woman was totally weird. I was also worried that I wouldn't get as much attention, but at least I had Mum all to myself and we weren't totally forgotten by the others. My sisters visited every week and still do, but it will never be the same because they didn't support us enough when times were hard at the beginning. My stepsisters and stepbrother come to visit too. To begin with, I used to run upstairs to my room to hide when they arrived and didn't come out until they had gone.

I had to come out of hiding when Mum went to Pakistan on her own for seven months. I was anxious because I'd thought Sameera was like a wicked stepmother and I was stressed out, thinking, what if Dad doesn't like me anymore? What if they leave me out? But they didn't, they treated me exactly as if I was one of them. As soon as I got there, my stepbrother Wajid asked how come I was never there whenever they visited me at home. I lied and told him I'd spent most of my time in hospital because I'd got cancer and the doctors were trying to figure out what to do with me. I had to come up with something that wouldn't offend him, didn't I? And guess what? The little idiot believed me for about a month and tried not to upset me because he thought I was dying. Dad found out, and one night while we were having dinner he asked outright, 'Do you have cancer or not?' I couldn't lie to him, could I? So I told them the truth. I couldn't believe how relieved they all were.

After that, I actually started to have some fun. We all began to act like a real family. It felt really good to be with my sisters, brother, Dad and new Mum – yes, I even began to see Sameera as a mother. My stepbrother, stepsisters and I became really close, closer than I've ever been with my sisters. We're nearer in age and like to do the same things – going shopping together and playing games. I love cricket and always insist that we play it at least once or twice when we're together. Except for cricket, I always lose games and they tease me, but I even like that!

When my mum came back, I didn't really want to part from the new family I'd joined and go to my single parent. So I was kind of mixed up. I wanted to cry and for a while I thought it would be like going through the divorce all over again – but it wasn't.

Every day I pray to my Allah, during Namaz (the prayer we do five times a day), that nothing bad happens to my mum and nothing will happen to part us. I find Eids pretty difficult; they are Muslim celebrations that happen twice a year where families get together, the women cook nice food and everyone gets presents. I really want to spend them with my dad, but if I do it will mean that my mum will be on her own. I did celebrate Eid with my dad once because my mum went round to my cousin's house. It was really fun.

Now, as a fourteen-year-old teenager, I can't really imagine how life would be if both my parents were together, and most of my past with two parents seems like a dream. There are times when I lie down and try to remember what life was like before. I haven't told many friends in school, but one or two of them found out when they came round to my house and my mum told them – I wasn't too impressed by that. I don't want to talk to them about it all now. They might start feeling sorry for me and give me sympathy, which might just make me start crying again.

I have got most of my life sorted now, I spend week-ends round my dad's and weekdays with my mum. Dad's house is only a short bus ride away so it's easy for us to visit each other. It's fun. I've got my mum all to myself and we've become really good friends, and her friends are close to me too. I have learnt a big lesson from this experience. Instead of locking myself away from my troubles, I have learnt that if I face them and come out of hiding I can actually start having fun. Now I've got a reason to smile.

See You Then

Larraine Jackson

My dad lives with his new wife, who is young enough to be his daughter. It's a bit of a cliché – and she used to be his secretary!

I can't say that I hate his wife, because I don't, but I don't like her. She is very introverted and nervous and makes me feel on edge, so I'm not comfortable when I visit them, which seems a bit wrong. She tries to be friendly and I can tell that she wants me to like her, but all she ever talks about is school and what I'm going to do when I'm older. It's always the same boring subjects. And all they ever talk about when they're together is work, so I just get ignored.

My cat now lives at my dad's house. It used to be lively and a fighter, but now it's just spoilt. Every time my dad's wife talks to it all softly and gently I get so mad, especially as it's my cat. When I go down to my dad's now I won't stroke it. I don't know why, but I associate it with Mum and Dad splitting up.

Anyway, let me tell you the ins and outs of Mum and Dad's split. I was upstairs on my own one night while my parents were fighting downstairs. One of them shouted, 'At least we can split up on good terms.' That was the first I'd heard of it. Well, after five minutes of running around like a mad cow with BSE, not knowing what to think or how to feel, I finally calmed down. My mind was partly blank, partly so confused that I couldn't even begin to react. I was shocked. Later on that night I went to sleep, blanked it out of my mind and forgot about it.

After that night, life just seemed to go on as usual and so did my parents. I didn't think any more of it until our annual family holiday when Mum told me and my two brothers that 'Ma and Pa are splitting up.' No one seemed particularly bothered, or at least they didn't show it – maybe they were pretending to be okay. We were just told not to say anything to our dad as we weren't supposed to know. I wasn't really upset – not even shocked any more. To me, it wasn't real. Mum and Dad had just had an argument, that was all. At that moment I couldn't believe they would really split up.

Nobody said anything else about it on holiday. When we got back, I went round to my friend Sonia's house. The first thing I told her was that my mum had said that she and Dad were splitting up. She looked even more shocked than I felt. Her reply was, 'So are my parents.' That made me feel relieved. After all, I was going to be a normal teenager – I knew a lot of people in our village whose parents had split up. Up until then, Sonia and I had

93

been the odd ones out, now we were going to be the same as everyone else.

The thing that upset me the most was that Dad didn't tell us he was leaving. He must have thought he had three extremely stupid kids. After all, why would all his belongings be in boxes? We were even sent to the shop to get the boxes. Didn't we matter enough for him to tell us properly, instead of just running away and not really saying goodbye? I don't know whether I was more mad at myself for not saying anything or at my dad. What really hurts is that he didn't think we knew and if my mum hadn't told us we wouldn't have known until the day he left.

Joanna, a friend from school, came over to visit the day my dad was leaving. She didn't know anything about what was going on and her parents were still together. I casually kissed my dad on the cheek and waved goodbye as he pulled away in a hired van packed with his belongings. It was just like every other goodbye, like waving him off to work, 'see you then'. Not one tear entered my eyes. After 10 minutes, my friend asked where my dad had gone. I told her he had left us. She just looked at me strangely, she must have thought the way it happened and the way I reacted – or didn't react – was bizarre. I wasn't sad, I just felt really mad. And I wasn't going to be bothered if he couldn't be.

But from then on life seemed to fall apart. At first, it was hell living with my mum. At the time I thought I hated her, she was always in a foul mood. Of course, it was because her husband of 20 years had just left her, but being

14 years old I didn't think that. I was just a rebellious teenage girl, getting arrested and causing havoc.

At school things weren't great either. You know when you get a teacher who you don't get on with; you just want to play up and make their life hell? Well, my history teacher couldn't control us whatsoever so we used to play pranks. One day some friends and I put Vicks VapoRub under our eyes to make it look like we were crying. This wasn't such a good idea, because it was just after my parents had split up and I actually started to cry properly and I couldn't stop. The teacher wasn't impressed and as I was normally the ringleader she chucked me out. The next day, my head of year came in and started shouting at me in front of the whole class, 'Are you sure it wasn't the Vicks that had made you cry?'

'No,' I replied, 'actually it's because my parents have just split up.' She was so shocked her face dropped and she started to cry herself. We went into her office to talk about it all and after that I had it pretty easy at school.

My dad moved down south, supposedly not with his girlfriend, but within a month I spotted her contraceptive pills in his bathroom so she must have been staying there. The house he lived in was cold and empty and not very comfortable. Even his towels were hard, they felt like Brillo pads when I dried my face. Six months later, he bought another house with his girlfriend, and then they got married. I still talk to my dad but, like him, I don't make the effort. He expects high things of me and wants me to do well, which is fair enough, after all I am his daughter. But he doesn't take the trouble to get to know me as a person and I always notice when he does the wrong thing, like giving me a Teletubbies mug when I was 16!

I am now 18 and no longer live with my mum, as I've moved in with my boyfriend. I didn't move out of Mum's because we didn't get on. In fact, after about a year, when Mum got over the initial hurt of Dad leaving and I passed my difficult teenage stage, we got on really well. It's just that she decided to move down south where her family is and I wanted to stay up here.

Living with my boyfriend is sometimes difficult because I'm very conscious of what he's doing and I'm always questioning where he's been. I don't think it's because of him as a person that I find it hard to trust him, it's because of Dad leaving and the way he did it. My dad let me down, and what is there to stop anyone else doing it? So Mum and Dad's divorce made me into an insecure, nagging girlfriend – or maybe that's just my excuse.

Mother, Daughter, Friend

Stephanie Ashton

My resolve was instant, like a bullet. My family had ripped in two, separating my dad from us and I immediately felt the responsibility as the older daughter to take care of my mum. I loved Mum, of course; and she was beautiful, with shoulder-length, blond hair, blue eyes and a dazzling smile that my little sister inherited. I knew there would be problems with Dad gone, so I pledged to myself that I would take his place. To become a shoulder for Mum's tears, to become a friend as well as a daughter. I was only 11 years old.

That is exactly what happened. Every day, I made a point of expressing an interest in her and would always ask how her day had been. Along with my sister Rachel I'd make up short plays or dances to entertain Mum when she was down. These would usually involve Rachel dancing and me acting or singing. We grew closer and took care of each other. When small jobs around the house needed to be done, jobs that my dad used to do, Rachel and I did them. I can still recall showing my mum how to wash her car, something I had attempted to help my dad with. I poured a cap full of the car cleaning fluid into a bucket of warm water, and Mum shrieked at me because she thought it was bleach!

I found this time so horrible. I had to comfort my mum when she was crying, try to cope with my own pain and yet still I chose to share hers. Being a single-parent family all of a sudden, we had to learn how to be completely self-sufficient. Money wasn't the problem. Mum was a well-paid nursery teacher, and the mortgage was already paid off. The problem for all of us, but especially for Mum, was loneliness.

Mum's friends helped out and so did our relatives, but there is only so much support that anyone can give, and our family all lived miles away. It seems fair to say that there was very little support for Mum from anyone. I was well aware of this even then and it reinforced my desire to look after her. We couldn't even go to church any more, something we had done all my life, because my mum was always so distraught during the service. The times we went we'd sit at the back so that she wouldn't draw too much attention to herself when she started crying. I wanted to take that pain away from her more than I wanted mine to disappear. I wanted to be the perfect daughter. I still felt like a child, but I tried to be more mature when I was around my mum so that she would respect me, be proud of me, so that she would confide in me and love me enough to forget her loneliness. At those moments I would change for a while into a grown-up individual, capable of sympathy, humour, and, ultimately, fairly intelligent advice that she sometimes put to use. I felt closer to her than anyone else I'd ever known.

But then, for a second time, everything changed. My mum found a boyfriend.

I'd grown up, I now think, a little too fast. Perhaps I hadn't grown up so much as grown too big for my boots, but I thought I was mature. I thought that East 17 were the greatest band on earth, and was absolutely infatuated with their lead singer, Tony Mortimer. There were other sides to this path of discovery that my mum didn't like – drinking alcohol, going out late at night with people who smoked, caking myself in thick make-up and, least of all, my steadily growing *attitude*. At the age of 15 I believed I was old enough to go out and enjoy myself as if I were 18.

Now Mum had her boyfriend, she didn't need to confide in me any more. I felt like she didn't need *me* any more. So I went out searching for the friendship and attention that I missed, that I no longer believed I had with my mum. It sounds ridiculous now, but I truly believed my role in our family had been totally blanked out, that it was now being filled by someone else.

I liked her boyfriend; I didn't direct my resentment towards him but I did direct it at my mum. I would shout, answer back, point-blank refuse to do any jobs around the house regardless of how little effort was required. I was a madam, a bitch, and completely in-tolerable to live with. Even Rachel, then 13, would tell me to do more work; she ended up doing most of my share. Despite all this I couldn't see that I was in the wrong, so I didn't make any effort to change. I think this is what prompted my mum to throw me out.

Saying 'throw me out' sounds as dramatic as it felt at the time – but in reality I returned within a couple of hours. This happened several times. The worst occasion was one evening at the beginning of autumn; I can't remember the exact time, only that it was cold and dark. A green car drove past me three times, and I was shivering and scared; tears endlessly streaming as I walked aimlessly for over two hours. I did a lot of thinking in that time, but my thoughts were clouded with excuses and self-justification. I couldn't appreciate the parenting, guidance, authority side of this mother–daughter relationship, and couldn't reconcile it with the friendship that we had shared. It felt like one moment my mum would be having a friendly chat with me about what happened last night, and the next she'd be telling me to tidy my room. I had felt like we were equals, forgot she was my mum as well as a friend, that she held the authority in the relationship. So I refused to accept my role as daughter, or even to compromise. When she began to confide in me less because she had Mark, well, that made me feel used, betrayed.

I put my mum through hell during this time, and I have never managed to explain why. I don't think I really cared about my attitude at home until I got my mock GCSE results. I had only passed three out of nine subjects with a C grade or above, yet I knew deep down that I was most definitely capable of doing much better. I hadn't revised for the mocks, I'd told my mum that I was revising in my room when I was secretly reading magazines. Suddenly I was afraid. I had done badly in the practice exams and the thought of doing no better in my real GCSEs was terrifying. By that time, the Easter before my GCSE examinations, I had made some new friends; good people who were fun to go out with as well as talk to. I encouraged myself to try really hard with school work, revised nightly, but, best of all, I slowly began to make an effort with my mum.

It is odd now, reflecting on all of those feelings, because so much has changed. My relationship with my mum has improved greatly; we're not as close as we were but I know that one day we shall be closer than ever before. I now listen to what she tells me, and while we don't always agree there is a lot of respect between us, which helps us to find compromises. I still attempt to entertain her with short plays as I'm in my final year of an A level in theatre studies. My music taste has thankfully developed beyond East 17! I now like soul.

I managed to pass eight of those nine GCSEs with good grades, something that gives me hope for every aspect of life. It has taught me a very valuable lesson, one which I continue to put to use with my mum even today at 19 – no matter what happens, so long as effort is put in, so much can be gained. Even my heart, which had turned to stone, learnt to beat again.

Swopping Places

Sarah Butler

People split up all the time. They grow apart or meet someone better or simply fall out of love. A basic fact, something I am well aware of, having split up enough times myself and nursed enough friends through broken hearts. But 'people' is not supposed to mean my parents. People is supposed to mean teenagers who are too young to be tied down. People is supposed to mean twenty-three-year-olds who rushed into marriage for the wrong reasons. People is supposed to mean craggy old strangers who'd spent the last 30 years screaming blue murder at one another. Nice, settled adults with good jobs, pretty houses and sensible children – adults just like my parents – are not supposed to be included.

Looking back, there were cracks. At the age of six, I overheard my parents agreeing, 'We'll stay together as long as the girls are at school.' At the age of seven, my father began advising me not to get married in my twenties, like they did, preferably never to get married at all. They hid the fights from my sister and me, but we noticed the sulky silences, the irritated sighs, heard them snapping, 'Hurry up – dinner's ready', 'Will you get off that computer!', 'Well, why don't you fix it, then?'

They would never have argued in front of us, they always tried their hardest to make things seem perfect, but sometimes the words would come out slightly too harshly, a comment would be slightly too barbed. We didn't miss a thing.

I always thought my parents were a strange match – my father wanted freedom and travel; my mother was quite content with her home comforts and close family ties. They never really socialised together. Despite all this they were mostly comfortable together and surely that was enough? Apparently it wasn't.

The split was long and subtle. My dad went about it in the same way my friends and I always seem to do. We put more distance between us and our partners, spend less and less time together, are less affectionate with them. We give ourselves time to think things through, assess the state of the relationship; we give our partners a chance to do the deed for us. We always feel heartless and cowardly throughout the whole thing, stringing them along because we're scared they might cry. It was vaguely disappointing to see that my dad was doing things the same way – moving to take up a new job, getting involved in lots of social activities in his new town, avoiding going home – but it also reminded me that he's human, and I knew that he'd thought it through. He wasn't just breaking my mother's heart on an impulse.

I was living 200 miles away, at university in Edinburgh, and was having to piece the clues together over the telephone. My mother spoke of visits cancelled or cut short, her feeling of losing touch with Dad. With both him and me gone, and my sister Nicky talking about moving out, she no longer knew what to do with herself, she spoke of long evenings in front of the television. My father talked about all his exciting new hobbies – cinema going, photography, doing up his (supposedly temporary) flat – enthused about his wonderful new friends, barely mentioned Mum at all. It wasn't hard to see that something was going wrong.

Nicky was right in the middle of it all, watching my parents' uncomfortable silences and my mother's distress following each visit from my father. Her reaction was different from mine, based on raw emotions and gut instinct. Distance allowed me to rationalise things and try to see both sides. Perhaps more cynical about relationships and commitment, thanks to my father's early warnings, I was willing to see that this could be for the best. Nicky, who has a more hopeful view of love, was not.

Nicky likes to believe marriage is for ever. She thinks if two people are right for each other they can make it work, and that our parents were throwing away 24 years of marriage needlessly. She could see how upset our mother was and couldn't believe Dad would put her through that; Mum and Dad get along well enough, so why did they have to go changing things?

Nicky is on Mum's side, but, at the same time, she's trying to avoid being around her. The family has always been Mum's life, and now that it's crumbling she's clinging to Nicky more than ever. She wants to know every detail of Nicky's life, spend all her free time with her and discuss the minute details of her married years. So Nicky is just trying to get out of the house at every opportunity; the sudden change from her and Mum screaming at each other about Nicky's Friday-night habits – messing around with boyfriends and sneaking into bars underage – to them discussing the most intimate matters is freaking her out. Mum is supposed to try to discipline her, bring her up properly. She is not supposed to be her friend.

I, too, am suddenly hearing a lot more from Mum. Dad, uncomfortable discussing private matters with anybody and especially his children, only calls me sporadically; it's not uncommon to go without contact for over a month. When we do talk, we tend to stick to relatively safe subjects – his job, my degree, books, films and TV programmes. Mum calls every couple of days, and it's getting to the stage where, guilty as it makes me feel, I'm beginning to dread talking to her.

Mum is still trying to figure out what went wrong and why she didn't notice earlier. She knows I'm more similar to Dad than to her, and she wants me to give her the answers. She can spend hours quizzing me about whether or not I know Dad's reasons, whether or not I saw this coming, whether or not I've spoken to him recently. If I admit to even 30 seconds on the phone with dad she needs to know what was said, every single word, and any hidden meanings.

Nicky feels disloyal to Mum if she phones Dad, and she's still not sure if she can forgive him. Mum and Dad have severed all but the most basic, necessary communication. I, thanks to my distant location, have become the family go-between. If Dad wants to know what Nicky's up to or how Mum's coping, he phones me. If Mum wants information on the break-up or to beat herself up about how happy Dad is, she phones me. My own news has become an almost forgotten polite enquiry tacked on the end of the phone call.

I don't really resent any of this. I know their reactions are only to be expected, only natural. But somehow it seems strange because they're my parents. If a friend needs convincing that splitting up is the best thing for them, I'll be there proclaiming, 'Do what makes you happy! Put yourself first! You deserve it!' Saying that to my dad means telling him it's fine to upset my mother. If a friend is distraught at having been dumped, I'll offer them Kleenex and tell them their partner was a git and they're better off free. But how can I tell my mum that my father is an undeserving slimeball? I don't even believe it myself.

This is the hardest part for both Nicky and me, the way the separation has changed all the familial roles. All through childhood you are allowed to believe that your parents are infallible, that no matter how upset you are or how much trouble you are in, you will be able to go to them and they will give you good advice. Parents are supposed to be strong and supportive, they are supposed to be united against anyone who might hurt you. They are not supposed to have any problems.

But suddenly they do.

Suddenly our parents are pulling their secure world apart. They are facing experiences they don't know how to deal with (and that Nicky and I, armed with our eventful romantic pasts, do). Suddenly they have problems, have doubts, are heartbroken or lonely. All the things they are supposed to help us with. Effectively, we have taken over their roles. Nicky is playing my mother's fiercely supportive part; I am the rational adviser my father always was. Where Nicky used to be emotional, crying and screaming and slamming doors, my mother has taken over; where I used to be the independent one, going off and living my own secret life of books and writing and friends they had never met, my father now has that role.

Of course, I want my parents to be happy in the long run, and if that means splitting up, then so be it; but watching your parents going through exactly the same emotions as breaking-up teenage friends is disconcerting. It can be hard to abandon childhood habits and to give them the support they deserve, but, ultimately, I grudgingly admit, they are entitled to have lives, too, with all the heartbreak and doubts and freedom that that entails.

From Russia with Love

Esther Bailey

I had promised my dad that the next time he went to Russia I would go with him, to see the new life he's made for himself, but I managed to keep the 'next time' in the future until I was trapped without escape. The thought of going to a place that I didn't know, to meet people who were important to my dad but unfamiliar to me, was daunting. Even before I knew that he and Mum would split up, when he was working out there, I had felt the same. Now, with the added emotional aspect, I knew it would be a difficult holiday.

Finally, two summers ago, I ran out of good reasons not to take Dad up on his kind offer of a free holiday. Rather expensive emotionally, though, as facing fears head-on is never easy. And so it was that I found myself sitting in my room in tears, the night before I was leaving, wondering if I really was grown-up enough to face the part of Dad's life I knew nothing about.

For me, accepting that there are parts to Dad that I know nothing about is probably more difficult than accepting that my parents are no longer together. That experience is all a bit of a haze, but now I am left with the realisation that the dad I thought I knew as I grew up, who was one of the people I could trust most, was someone else entirely. And so began the painful time of revalidating our relationship. To me, each deception cost a memory; I could no longer think of our past times with joy, even though so many of them were good. That is why I decided to go to Russia with him, not because I particularly wanted to, but because I knew that to regain our shared history I needed to accept and embrace what had become most important to him.

That was the theory – not so easy in practice! We met in the morning at Mum's house, and after a difficult goodbye with Mum I stepped out into the Great Unknown. The first challenge came as soon as we left the airport, as Dad's new partner was driving; and not only that but she was driving the car which, for a while, I had considered my own. Far too symbolic for seven o'clock in the morning.

I was full of apprehension when I arrived in Russia, as I knew that I would be treated with great respect and welcomed by the people I was nervous about meeting. I didn't know if they had any idea of Dad's life in England, or how difficult it was for me to be there. Dad and I spent the first couple of days together, seeing the surroundings, talking, laughing and meeting some of his colleagues. Not so hard, I began to think, maybe there's not so much to this 'accepting' game. In fact, the times we spent together during those days were some of the best we'd had for years.

However, once the business week started and I was no longer the only person to see, I felt that I effectively disappeared from his schedule. Meeting person after person whose name I had heard and whose face I recognised from the many photos Dad brought back from previous trips would have been a lot easier if I could speak Russian. I found myself repeatedly asking, why could Dad not have found friends like this for himself at home? But knowing that these people were important to Dad made me swallow my pride and try to get to know them.

However, as the week progressed I began to feel very lonely. Not through lack of company, but because I felt isolated, both by the language barrier and the struggle going on inside me. While Dad was in meetings I was taken around the city by friends of his, who were generous beyond their means. It was a strange feeling, knowing that under any other circumstances I would be happy to meet such friendly and welcoming people, but that under these circumstances every new person presented a challenge.

I inevitably ended up spending every night sitting alone in the flat wondering where Dad was. I longed for someone to talk to, to tell just one person I'd met what I was really feeling, that I wasn't there on holiday, that I wasn't enjoying it as much as I would have them believe. I felt like a true outsider.

I knew that some of the people I met had had affairs with Dad, and I found that difficult. But although my immediate reaction was to feel hostile and unfriendly, I could hear a little voice inside reminding me that this was how Dad chose to live his life, and that I had no right to take that away from him.

Accepting Dad's partner, who now lives in England, is not easy. I still keep her very much at arm's length. Communication is not easy as her English is fairly restricted, but all in all it is simply an awkward relationship, which may change with time.

All of this said, I keep returning again and again to the fact that I cannot dictate Dad's life. Yes, it hurts. Everyone who has experienced family break-up knows just how much it hurts, how the basis for everything you thought you could trust is suddenly swept from beneath your feet, and how confusing even the smallest thing can become. It's learning to move on from that point which I think is important, learning to forgive and trying your best to forget.

I said at the beginning that I wanted to accept and embrace those things that Dad feels are important. My trip to Russia did not achieve that. I cried for days when I got home, and it was all I could do not to cry for the last few days I was there, knowing that Dad has a whole life of which I am simply not a part. The truth is that I have lost the dad I grew up with.

What I have gained, though, is the dad I now have. Being in Russia, walking on the privileged ground of his secret life, if you like, made me realise just how much I have to let Dad be Dad, that I have to accept him for who he is, just as he let me make my mistakes when I was growing up and yet always let me come back to him.

Forgiveness is an active process, which sometimes I have to do time and again, but it's worth it. It makes the pain of remembering what's gone before more bearable, and gives you something to work with in the present.

Contributors' Notes

Stephanie Ashton is now 19 and plans to do an English and Drama degree next year. She enjoys socialising with her friends as well as staying in with a good film and pizza, but she hates getting up the next day.

Esther Bailey is 23 and studying at Canterbury University. She is getting married later this year, and hopes she has learnt from her parents' experience. If she had any free time she would love to travel more, but she makes do with the odd trip to Margate! She enjoys good times and good food with her friends.

Samantha Bradfield is 21 and trying to get through university – very slowly! She spends her life obsessing about music and worshipping the Manics. When she grows up she wants to be famous. Until then, she will just play at being the ultimate messed up rock chick. It's fun.

Bonna Breeze is 18 and currently teaching English in Russia for six months, before going to university to study philosophy. Back in England, she lives with her mother and younger sister in north Yorkshire. Bonna loves to read, sing and play melodeon when she's not out with her mates.

Sarah Butler is 21 and has just graduated from Edinburgh University. At present, she is unemployed and sleeping on friends' sofas, but she prefers not to worry about the details. She loves watching films, and is a fan of directors Kevin Smith and Hal Hartley. She enjoys practising astrology, and wants to be a writer.

Zaynah Farsian is 19 years old and lives in London. She is of Indian heritage and is the oldest of four children. She lives with her mother and siblings, and is currently studying for her A levels. Her father moved out when she was 13, but she doesn't feel like something is missing, because of the constant support from her mother's side of the family. She loves to read books of all genres, and enjoys playing basketball and badminton, watching films and listening to music.

Monique Ferguson is 18 years old and she lives with her mum, stepdad, brother and stepbrother. She's had asthma since she was 14, which means that she goes into hospital every few months. She's into archery in a big way and she is hoping to go to uni soon to study law. She hates Monday mornings and people who won't let you be who you want to be.

Harriet Flynt is 17 and is presently studying for her A levels. She lives with her mum and one of her older brothers, who are always nagging her to 'get off the phone and do some homework'. She is applying to go to drama school, hoping to be trained as a professional actor and perhaps work with her hero, Gary Oldman! Harriet plays the clarinet, piano, saxophone, guitar and sings. She likes listening to music and going out with her friends. She hopes that she will one day see her name in lights and have to fight the press off her front door!

Sarah Fowler is 19 and is currently studying for a literature degree at Liverpool University. She still lives at home with her mum, older brother and sister. In her spare time she works at a cinema and also enjoys watching films and reading. Her older sister Stephanie has also contributed a piece for this book.

Stephanie Fowler is currently working for a shipping company in Merseyside, and is still hoping for a decent career in writing, plus a season ticket at the Kop at Anfield. She is living at home with her mum, brother and sister, Sarah (see above). Her passions include music, film, books, clubs, Anfield and football, football, football.

Emma Harris is 16 years old. She lives with her mum in the Midlands. Her father lives close by and she visits him and his new family from time to time. She loves garage music and goes clubbing with her friends. She's mad about 'How Deep is Your Love' by Dru Hill and plays it all the time. She can't stand it when people whisper. She wants to be a fashion journalist.

Larraine Jackson is 18 years old and lives in Nottinghamshire. She is interested in sport and fitness as well as going out clubbing – although they don't tend to mix. At the moment she is studying A levels at college, hoping to pass and study leisure centre management next year. She was born in Germany when her father was in the army there, then they moved to Nottinghamshire where she has stayed, but over the years her mum, her dad and two brothers have moved away.

Sara Jenkins is 22 years old and lives with friends in north London. Her flat is close to her older brother, which she is glad about as they haven't lived so near to each other since she was 13. She recently graduated with a degree in sports science from Liverpool University and is now looking to get into TV/film production or to be a climbing instructor. Her parents divorced when she was 18. After the divorce her father moved to Spain – which is handy for a cheap holiday, but Sara finds it hard being so far away from him. She speaks to her mum every day – she's her best friend.

Chloe Johnson is 14 and lives with her mum and her stepdad. Her dad moved out when she was seven and she goes to see him every other weekend. She has three step-brothers and two sisters. She is studying for her GCSEs. She wants to be a successful violinist when she is older, and loves folk music and being with her best friend.

Ruby Khan is 14 and lives with her mum in north London. She loves reading historical novels and particularly likes anything written about the English Civil War. Ruby is also mad about cricket; she watches it on telly whenever she gets the chance and, like her dad, she supports Pakistan. She started playing the game herself while on holiday in Pakistan, where it is a popular game for girls – she classes herself as a good fast bowler!

Melanie O'Brien is 13 years old and lives in north London with her mum, her twin brother and older sister (aged 16). She is a keen actress – she goes to three drama groups, and also likes playing steel pans for a steel band. She can read for hours on end. She finds it very frustrating when people go in and out of friendships from one day to the next.

Cat Reilly is now 17 and lives in a small town in the Lake District with her mum and her mum's partner. She is an only child and isn't sure if it's a blessing or not! She likes punk/rock music and having a good time with her friends. Living life to the max is definitely a high priority although school work and being successful are up there too. She doesn't like mean people or unhappiness and thinks everyone should try to reach their potential.

Isaaka Wesley is 16 years old and lives in a children's home. She hasn't seen her stepmother for two years but is still in touch with her stepbrother. She is a thinker and spends a lot of time alone reading, watching TV or writing poetry. She has done some performance poetry, which was so nerve-racking it made her shake all over –

but she still enjoyed it! She likes talking to close friends on the phone and loves the book *The Color Purple* and the film *Waiting to Exhale* – mainly because they portray strong black women.

Rebecca Woollard grew up in France and in a small town in Cambridgeshire. Her parents split up when she was 12 and Rebecca continued to live with her mum and brother before leaving home to go to university. She now works in London, but is very close to her mum. She likes going to clubs, socialising with friends, and is a voracious reader.

Resources

Child's Eye
231 Camberwell New Road
London SE5 0TH
Tel 020 7701 1114 or 020 7703 2532
Free counselling for children and teenagers up to the age
of 16 on any aspect of family break-up and stepfamilies.
This service covers London. Give them a ring to find out
about other services around the country.

ChildLine
Tel 0800 1111
A free 24-hour telephone line for any child/teenager who
is worried about anything, including family break-up.

Citizens Advice Bureau
Will tell you what services exist for young people in your
area. Check your telephone directory for the nearest.

Gingerbread

16–17 Clerkenwell Close
London EC1R 0AN
Phone free on 0800 0184 318
Phone for a free copy of Junior Ginger – a magazine for children and young people who live in a one parent family.

National Council for One Parent Families

255 Kentish Town Road
London NW5 2LX
Phone free on 0800 0185 026
Produces a guide to fiction that includes one parent family scenarios – for children and young people.

Parentline Plus (used to be called Stepfamily)

520 Highgate Studios
53–79 Highgate Road
London NW5 1TL
Tel 020 7284 5500
www.parentlineplus.org.uk
Contact them for free leaflets on coping in a stepfamily.

Relateen

Provides counselling to teenagers whose parents have split up. To find out whether a Relateen service exists in your area contact Relate on 01788 573 241.

The Who Cares? Linkline

Tel 0500 564 570
A free helpline for young people in care who want to talk about anything that is bothering them, such as family contact.